YOU CAN CHANGE your personality- and your life

YOU CAN CHANGE your personality- and your life

Kurt Haas

Nelson-Hall ⬚nh⬚ Chicago

Library of Congress Cataloging in Publication Data

Haas, Kurt.
    You can change your personality-and your life.

    Includes index.
    1. Success.   2. Personality change.   I.   Title.
BF637.S8H18   158'.1   78-11449
ISBN 0-88229-429-6

Manufactured in the United States of America

10   9   8   7   6   5   4   3   2   1

contents

One

What, Why, and How

Pause! For a moment think about the person you want to be. Let your fantasy roam and freely imagine the changes you want to make in yourself. Think about those things in you that you do not like and want to be rid of. Consider also the traits you would like to add to your personality and your life. The instructions for this assignment are simple: hold nothing back. No matter how silly or trivial it may seem, include in your self-inventory everything that involves any change in your conduct, habits, behavior, or character. Most important, do not forget those changes you have always wanted to make but about which you have become discouraged. We know that nearly all of us have tried in very many ways to be different, yet, despite our efforts, have sooner or later failed. So, in the list of hoped-for changes, be certain to include every hope and resolution, no matter how small it may seem, or how difficult.

Write down, or mentally catalogue, all the changes you want to bring about in yourself before reading further. Do this now, because the experiences of other people, described next, could influence your own judgements. After you have thought of everything you have always wanted to be, read on.

The great majority of people, when asked about how they want to change, are not optimistic, but they are down-to-earth. No one really demands eternal beauty, total happiness, or self-perfection. Nearly everyone states goals that are within reach, though they themselves have somehow never been able to reach

1

them. Consequently, they have become discouraged about their chances for ever improving themselves. They have tried and failed so often they are convinced that they have little or no will-power, or just bad luck. Here are some typical examples of what people say.

> I would like to have a lot more ambition. I want to be more aggressive and not give up so easily. But I have tried and it just does not seem to work. I have made so many resolutions to push harder, but I just don't seem to be able to keep it up.

> I want to be less afraid. I'm too fearful of so many things. I could recite you a list of a baker's dozen. And I worry too much. If it's not this, it's that. But I just can't change. I have tried, but I can't do it. I cannot control my fears.

Some people when describing what they want, try to give up traits or roles they believe have been forced on them. They may say, "I want to stop wearing a mask and be myself." They may express a desire to no longer "put up with being just a wife, just living the life that husband and parents want." A young husband felt that most of his life he had been forced to assume a character role that was totally false. He put it this way:

> Everyone has always treated me like a clown. It's some-thing I let them do, maybe even encouraged them, since I was a kid. I guess I had to play that part to get along. It was my adjustment you might say. But it's not me! I have a lot of anger in me. I am not a nice guy. I'm not good-natured! I could be a street fighter or be in some resistance movement or something. I am very serious, and I have very deep feel-ings about the things that go on. I want to be able to show my feelings when I'm mad or I'm disgusted. I want to be taken seriously!

Many self-changes that are desired actually involve others. Perhaps we want to be more affectionate, less argumentative, or able to freely enjoy different sexual experiences. All of these needs involve friends, spouses, or other people.

> I want to truly experience love. I want someone to love me deeply with very intense feeling and I want to be able to love them back in the same way. People say I am a very cold person but it's not true. I can love, if I had a chance. I know I can.

When we look over the wishes of others, and our own assortment of desires, it is easy to become discouraged. Some plans involve changing habits that have lasted for thirty or forty years or more, ever since earliest childhood. Other people, such as the man attempting to be more serious, try to add on personality traits that have never been part of them at all in any way. Even more complex, and therefore seemingly even more improbable, are the plans to make self-changes that actually include others. It may be a tough chore just to try to change ourselves, but is it even possible to bring about modifications affecting others? After all, if our ambition is to stop being afraid of crowds, or to build up our ability to make decisions, we need to work only with our own personality. But if our aim is to establish harmony with our husband (or wife), be deeply loved, or to try new erotic activities, we require someone else to cooperate.

When the behavior that we want to alter involves others, the process can be intricate and the progress very gradual. Modifying personal interactions can also require subtle and persistent techniques somewhat different from those we use just to bring about changes in ourselves alone. But all the changes sought by the persons described in the preceding pages are possible, and the chances are excellent that so, too, are all the goals you have personally listed at the beginning of this chapter. Whether the alteration we want to bring about is in just a simple habit, whether it consists of a more profound characteristic, or touches upon the lives of several others, it can be done.

We are aware that if you have thought about or written down your own aspirations you have painfully recalled how frustrating your efforts have been in the past. All of us have an uneven history of trying to be different. Whether prompted by the criticism of others, by New Year's resolutions, or by native good sense, most of us have attempted to change and failed. But these past failures do *not* forecast the future. Most self-change efforts almost have to fail. They are uninformed and so haphazard that they inevitably fizzle out. Take, for instance, the man who felt he needed more ambition. Frequently, he berated himself for being lazy, not trying hard enough, or having too little courage. Over and over, he resolved to "stick it out." Sometimes he even planned elaborate campaigns, rehearsing every step, so that he would be thoroughly prepared for his next challenge. But though he occasionally seemed to have some success, most of the time he tired of his resolve and consoled himself with several drinks.

Another example of the typical uninformed attempt to bring about significant change, this time involving more than one person alone, was revealed by the woman who felt she wanted to find love. By inclination, she was distinctly introverted. She disliked parties and found it difficult to make small talk or be casual. In addition, she resented having to dress "just to attract a man," and preferred to be clothed in jeans and sweaters and not wear any kind of makeup. But every once in a while, prompted by her own frustration or the cynical comments of relatives, in her search for love she started a round of superficial intimacies. She tried to reverse every aspect of her character, to be carefree and outgoing, and as a result did manage to surround herself temporarily with a few male friends. But all too soon, and invariably, each burst of extroverted energy ended in disappointment. Love, as she wanted it, continued to elude her. The young husband who tired of playing clown had similarly disappointing experiences. His friends and his wife were so accustomed to laughing at his comments that, when he tried to show his seriousness or rage, they merely thought he was being extra funny.

It is the experience of the majority that efforts at self-change fail. Very few persons, on their own, manage to reshape their existence. Consider again the list of changes that you want to bring about for yourself. If you are like most, your objectives are far from extravagant and, potentially, highly attainable. Yet, you too, though you have made several earnest efforts to change have never quite reached your goals. But though few have succeeded on their own, and herein lies *the purpose of this book*, nearly everyone can *learn* to change his or her personality and life.

Willpower, Guilt, and Pessimism

Since we have tried in the past to be different and our efforts to change ourselves and our situations have failed, it is easy to be pessimistic. "I guess I am too old to change." "I heard this woman say that her psychiatrist said your personality is laid down in childhood and afterwards there is nothing you can do about it." The truth is that there is no age limit or time barrier to almost any modification we want to make within ourselves. A sixty-three-year-old man sexually unresponsive for five years taught himself to be totally functioning again—in fact, more vigorous than ever before. A woman afraid of crowds, restaurants, insects, and many other things for over twenty years, managed slowly and steadily to overcome each fear.

There is no reason to be pessimistic about our chances for changing just because we have failed in the past. Neither do we have to be pessimistic because we have somehow come to falsely believe that it is too late to modify our adult lives. Despite what we think, may have read, or heard, personality is *not* irrevocably shaped in childhood. Our character and our destiny are *not* forever molded in infancy or, at the latest, before the age of six.

There is no age at which new learning and change is impossible. We can grow and develop psychologically for all of our lives. The noted psychoanalyst, Erik Erikson, long with Harvard University, has pointed out that each stage in life, including adulthood and old age, can be critically examined by ourselves and subject to our will to change. We are not fated to remain forever what we were as children. Each passing year offers the alert individual new opportunities and new potentials.

Even worse than feeling pessimistic about our own prospects for change is to be possessed by guilt. We try and fail, try and fail again, and each time feel more and more guilty. Ultimately we give up, sheepishly admitting a lack of willpower. "I tried to stop being so disorganized [lazy or timid] but I just don't seem to have any willpower." "I tried to be more independent [honest, assertive, or cooperative], but something always seems to happen that messes up my resolutions." In truth, however, just as age is not the cause of our lack of success neither is poor willpower. Nearly all attempts at self-change fail because our efforts are unguided, inadequately motivated, and usually totally unorganized.

We cannot expect to know how to fly an airplane by just sitting in the cockpit and willing it. In the same way, we cannot just fumble and tinker with our character and resolve to be different. Flying, ice-skating, or speaking Italian involves learning and so does becoming more ambitious, cooperative, loving, sexy, or tranquil. Turning this around, it becomes easy to see that if we were plunked into a cockpit and urged to use our willpower to get us off the ground, of course, all our efforts would fail. And, of course, we would not blame ourselves or our willpower for not getting us up in the air. We do not feel guilty about not knowing how to fly because we have never learned. Similarly we have every legitimate right to stop blaming ourselves for past unsuccessful efforts at personality change. No one has ever taught us how to change.

We can *stop feeling guilty* about our failure to change for we have simply never been taught what to do. And we do need to get rid of this guilt, for it, by itself, is an impediment to future change. The more we dwell on our past, the more we berate ourselves for alleged past weaknesses, errors, or shortcomings, the harder we make the process of change. Each of us awakes each day a potentially new person, and we need not carry around with us old, self-imposed psychological blemishes. Often as not, it is our own stubborn insistence on burdening ourselves with every failure from our past that actually prevents us from trying and succeeding in the present. This was insightfully explained by a man who had spent more than twelve years in jail.

> The reason I failed twice before and went back to jail is the same, I think, for every ex-con. Any man that has been incarcerated comes out and says to himself, "I'm no good." "I'm a failure, a has-been and I cannot keep out of trouble." So right then and there they are predicting trouble for themselves. They just believe it has to be. What made the difference in me is I said to myself this one day, "Today you are a new person. You are intelligent. You have learned a trade. You can be as happy as you let yourself be or you can continue to think of yourself as nothing." So I chose to be a new person. I am something. I am someone else and my whole new life lies ahead of me. All my failures in the past are past. The past is gone. I am new and today is a new day.

The only way to break through the vicious cycle of low self-opinion, guilt, and pessimism is to recognize that willpower, diehard resolve, and determined ironclad ambition have far less to do with change than simple learning. Want to drive a car? Take a few lessons and read a good driver-education manual. Want to speak Italian? Get a good tutor. Want to change your personality and your life? Learn the three critical steps: *What, Why,* and

How. First we need to know exactly what it is that we want to accomplish. Next we have to understand the why: our own motives that will assist (or sabotage) our efforts. And finally, we need to know how: the techniques to bring about self-change we desire.

What

What, in the most specific terms, is it that we actually want to change about ourselves? We may say we want to be more loving, aggressive, or independent, but precisely what do we mean? When we describe the changes we desire, we need to carefully avoid using generalizations or vague adjectives. Words such as *lazy, ambitious, sexy, independent,* and *courageous* have meaning for us only when we can clearly understand the behaviors they describe. It is difficult and misleading to work toward a goal that is a verbal abstraction. Few of us can agree among ourselves what is intended by such words as *honest, confident,* or *mature.* But, if we say we want to be able to face a job interview without perspiring, being tongue-tied, or at a loss for words, all of us can understand our objectives.

The *What* necessitates that we elaborate in the most specific, concrete terms what it is that we actually want to change. Instead of saying we want to be more self-reliant or independent we will have to give numerous examples of the actual behavior we seek. Here are two different persons describing just some of the behaviors they have labeled independence.

> I want to be able to travel alone, without having to take any friend along for moral support. I want to be able to live in my own place, alone, cook alone, clean, eat alone, all that.
>
> For me independence means making my own decisions without asking my husband, or anybody, for help. I want the courage to live my own life. Stay out at night. Work during the day, and go to school again. I want to be able to have my own friends, not necessarily people my husband likes. I want to feel free to do what I want anytime I want to. I know that's a feeling and I'll try to define it better.

In Chapter Two, the means used to translate vaguely stated desires into behavioral specifics will be described. We will learn that the first critical step in self-change is to pinpoint as clearly as possible what exactly it is that we want to change. Often as not we will find, as a result of our specification, that the more vividly we describe our objectives in behavioral terms, the more attainable our goals become.

Why (and Willpower)

The step following *What* (exactly what it is we want) is the careful examination of our own motivation. We may say we want to be more loving and define it beautifully in terms of hugs, pats, smiles, and kisses. Yet when we probe our motivation, perhaps instead of uncovering a need to be affectionate, we may discover one for authority. It is for this reason, incidentally, that some people who think they want to experience love are unsuccessful in their quest. Very often such individuals are actually driven by needs such as dominance or control and, as a consequence, find all their relationships turn into unhappy power struggles.

When our motivation is not in harmony with the objectives we have planned, no matter how clear our aspirations or masterful our techniques, we will not attain our goals. Motivation is what most of us mean when we say willpower. We may know perfectly well how to go about reducing our fear of animals or the opposite sex but, unless we are truly motivated to do so, our efforts will be useless. In this sense, blaming our failure on inadequate willpower is correct. By saying our willpower is responsible for our lack of success we are stating we know that without strong and unequivocal motivation, any self-change project is a failure before it even starts. Notice that nowhere have we said that you must mobilize your willpower, marshall your motivation, and the like. It cannot be done. What we are saying is that you must know and understand your motivation. If it is in harmony with the behavioral goals you have set, everything will go well. But if an examination of your drives shows a conflict, it is time to rethink your objectives or even seek help concerning your motivation.

The conflict between motivation and behavioral objectives was well illustrated by the salesman who wanted to be more aggressive. He carefully worked out the *What*, neatly defining many situations in which he would call on more clients, stay with them longer, and be clearly informed and persuasive about his products. All in all, he worked out a list of several dozen such specific behaviors. Yet, when he tried to put his plans into operation, they never seemed to work out. When he attempted to sell longer and harder, he developed a headache and was forced to give up. He studied his products more carefully but did this so late at night that he was too tired to remember much the next day. He called on more clients but ended up chatting aimlessly so that he made even fewer sales. The one area in which he seemed, at first, to be more successfully aggressive was with his wife. He involved himself in a great many domestic interactions that required him to lead and demonstrate authority. Initially his spouse seemed to respond well to his new directness but gradually this situation also deteriorated. The result was that both the salesman's job and his marriage, instead of improving because of his supposed attempt to be more aggressive, were getting much worse.

What was wrong in this instance was nearly all traceable to motivation. This man felt himself stuck in an unhappy job and an incompatible marriage. To improve both, a relatively superficial investigation of his situation and character suggested he needed to work harder at the traditional masculine role of being aggressive. Luckily, when attempts at being aggressive failed, the salesman analyzed his motivation much more extensively. Soon his self-inquiry revealed that he was far more driven by dependency than by aggression. He wanted and needed situations in which he would be directed, cared for, led, and guided. In his work he could be very happy and successful if he were carefuly instructed in what to do. In his marriage he desired a strong woman who would nurture him, provide him with support and encouragement, and permit him to play a relatively passive role. This man wanted to change his life but not in the direction of aggression— when he attempted to be more aggressive, his conflicting motivation led him to fail. His willpower appeared weak, his behavioral efforts went astray, and he felt even more a failure, all because he did not clearly understand his own motives.

Personality change will continue to elude any person whose motivation is not supportive. We will continue to be unsuccessful and blame our willpower in our struggle to lose weight, or to be uninhibited, more affectionate, or more aggressive, as long as we do not clearly understand our innermost needs. In order to know our motivation, we will have to candidly examine all our biases, feelings, prejudices, and lifelong preconceptions. Often as not, we will have to probe ourselves very thoroughly, for many motives lie hidden within the unconscious. Frequently, major thoughts and feelings that control our lives are deeply buried and it takes considerable effort to become aware of them. The means we can use to explore, understand, and utilize our motivation will be discussed in Chapter Three.

How

We were not born lazy, fearful of crowds or the opposite sex, or argumentative and depressed. Certainly, genetic and other biologic conditions make some babies more easily content, brighter, or more responsive. But nearly all the behaviors we desire, or want to eliminate, have very little to do with biology but lots to do with learning. The chances are excellent that, if we are fearful, we learned to become so because of frightened parents or mismanaged traumatic experience. If we are inhibited or dependent, it may be the result of growing up in a negative, punitive household. Or if we are not as enthusiastic or affectionate as we desire, it is often a result of emerging from a home and milieu that denied us these qualities.

> Paul was a nice-appearing but very inhibited and withdrawn young man. He very much wanted to socialize with women but found his feelings of guilt made it difficult for him to even begin a conversation. He worked for a large firm and every Friday after work fifty to hundred young employees would congregate in a nearby lounge to drink, talk, and dance. There were always very many women there, but the few times Paul had gone he felt an absolute wallflower.
>
> Paul carefully analyzed his situation and worked out his ambitions in terms of specific behavioral objectives. By carefully observing the barroom scene Paul calculated that he did not actually need to do much talking since the lounge was so noisy. But he did need to smile and look at any new acquaintance. Hence, as a start in his effort to make himself more sexually adequate, he decided to smile and look at two different women the next time he went to the bar. Each smile and glance would have to last two seconds. After he completed his quota of contacts, he could treat himself to a

drink. Thereafter, in subsequent Friday afternoon bar visits, Paul would have to increase his quota of women smiled at and the length of each contact. Each time, he would not allow himself the reward of a drink till his behavioral goal was completed.

Paul is using a learning technique to teach himself to be less prudish and establish relationships with the opposite sex. There are a great many different ways in which all of us can teach ourselves the behaviors we want, or want to drop. Very often, a reinforcement program such as Paul employed in rewarding himself for "good" behavior results fairly quickly in important personality changes. In contrast, we may on occasion want to eliminate or modify some aspects of our personality and could do so by, in a sense, punishing those characteristics. Still another learning method is desensitization, which can help us overcome anxiety and fear. Or we may try even another approach to overcome blocks and psychological barriers. We may, in effect, erase all sorts of old biases and habits and with new information reprogram our personality.

This short description of the *How* may sound complex since it is compressed, but it is not actually difficult. In the chapters where the specific techniques are spelled out it will become apparent that we have been using all of these learning procedures, although unknowingly and inefficiently, all our lives. In many different ways, we have been taught by others and by ourselves, to become what we are, but, because we have not recognized what was happening, have had very little control over the process. Once we understand how we have learned, we will be able to unlearn and relearn, take control, and change our personalities and our lives.

Ethical Behavior

In the last decade, psychologists have become acutely aware that their understanding and explanation of how people learn generate very powerful tools for change. Techniques such as reinforcement, token systems, desensitization, and reciprocal inhibition can bring about profound changes in individual behavior. Unfortunately the entertainment media have played up the most negative aspects of these learning processes. Dozens of stories of the mad manipulation of mind and behavior have been highly popular. The impression can easily be obtained that psychologists are lurking in the shadows able and ready to turn individuals into brainless robots whose heads can be precisely controlled in any way their scientific masters wish. Dramas such as those presented on television and in the movies are gross and frivolous exaggerations. But there is a small kernel of truth in that knowledge about shaping behavior can be properly used or abused. Teachers, leaders, governments can utilize our understanding of the techniques of learning to help create more decent, peaceful, freer, and self-actualized human beings. Or they can focus their efforts on bringing about people who are intolerant, pugnacious, and uncritically obedient.

Of most direct concern to us in changing our own behavior is that we make sure that our goals are ethical, consistent with the best feelings we have toward other men and women. Obviously we are not about to teach ourselves to be burglars, sadists, or swindlers. But we need to be careful that our self-directed changes do not subtly corrupt our own character or inflict serious hurt on others.

> Bart is a thirty-six-year-old married man and father of two young daughters. For the last several years he has been having secret affairs. He is a modestly successful lawyer, and nearly all his relationships have been with women who initially came to see him as clients. Bart complains that he is never fully able to enjoy his extramarital romances because he frequently feels guilty. He believes his guilt is a result of the fact that he is lying to his wife, using his authority position to impress and seduce his clients, and telling his mistresses that they mean more to him than they actually do. Bart neatly specified the behavioral objectives that would enable him to feel less guilty, more potent, carefree, and so on. He was also well motivated to learn to reduce these feelings and was already familiar with many learning techniques.

What ethical problems are involved, if any, in Bart's desire to feel less guilty? It is our contention that Bart himself, or a therapist working with him, should be concerned about his *source* of guilt. The person who feels guilty about masturbating, disobeying his parents, or changing jobs may well feel needless anxiety.

But the individual who feels guilty because he is being grossly dishonest to his wife and lovers, or is stealing tools from his employer, may need to carefully question his attitudes, and his standards for ethical behavior. We should not try to be psychologists, philosophers, puritans, moralists, or theologians. But we must have a commitment to ourselves not only to function competently but also to be better persons.

Bart's desire to be less guilt-stricken and anxious powerfully conflicts with the ethical goals of honesty and helpfulness. Notice we are not commenting on Bart's extramarital ventures themselves. Today there are many different marital styles. Our concern about Bart is not motivated by a naive belief that all marriages for everyone are sexually faithful. Many new and innovative marital and partnership arrangements, involving the willing consent of all participants, are working very well. Our criticism of Bart is directed at his lying, disregard for the feelings of his wife and his callous treatment of his mistresses. Bart does not need to learn to feel less guilty, he needs instead to learn how to communicate with his wife, establish rapport, be honest, and develop reciprocally satisfying relationships.

Whatever our personality wants are, we need to consider whether our behavior will hurt ourselves or others. Sometimes, of course, even the most worthwhile goals will cause a temporary hardship. For example, a twenty-four-year-old woman whose aim was independence included as one of her behaviors moving out of her parental home. While this resulted in considerable distress to her parents, it was a wholesome act, consistent with every traditional ethical prescription and ultimately beneficial to her own and to her parents continued growth. All of us attempting to change personality need to be constantly alert to the consequences of our conduct. Behaviors that involve dishonesty, manipulation, rationalization, malevolence, and the like must be diligently avoided. Overall, whatever changes that learning techniques help to bring about should respect the well-being of others.

Obtaining Help

Not all personality changes can be managed by the person

alone. Even the most complete book on learning techniques, psychotherapy, or other personal guidance is not an adequate substitute for people who require professional attention. Often, unfortunately, individuals who are seriously upset, frightened, depressed, and confused, are exceedingly suspicious or otherwise reluctant to seek help. They put off seeing a therapist, afraid they will be told they are ill and need treatment. A book such as this is not a substitute for expert care and should not be used as such. Any person who is markedly distressed or has wrestled with difficult emotional problems for a long time should get personal professional assistance.

An additional caution that is wise before starting any self-change project is to get a physical checkup. Sometimes what appears a behavioral objective may actually be a medical problem. One person who tried very diligently with a well-constructed relearning program to relieve his frequent bouts of depression nevertheless continued to fail. Finally, he sought the help of an internist who discovered his depression was totally physical. He had a thyroid deficiency that periodically caused him to feel depressed. Another individual had worked out a good program to help herself obtain greater sexual pleasure. Despite the fact that almost everything seemed to work well, she still had frequent bouts of vaginal pain and spasm. Here a gynecological examination revealed a hidden but chronic infection as the cause of her problem. For these reasons, it is well to seek medical help whenever there is any possibility of a physical difficulty.

Finally, it is important to realize that, despite contrary impressions, when psychologic help is required, it is readily available, likely to be reasonable in cost, and effective. In the majority of instances, treatment by a qualified psychologist or psychiatrist is not a prolonged ordeal but a relatively short and reasonable joint effort. Further, just like physical disorders, most emotional difficulties can be treated, many patients recover fully, and even those with the most serious difficulties show distinct improvements.

Two
What-
Defining
our
Goals

Our everyday speech is filled with abstract and imprecise words like *stingy*, *shy*, *jealous*, or *anxious*. As a result, we are vague when we describe our personal goals. We say we need "self-confidence" or are trying to be more "loving" or hoping for "ambition." But what do we really mean when we confess that we would like to be self-confident? Following are different interpretations of self-confidence from different people:

A twenty-four-year-old student said that self-confidence was the ability to stop hiding and "get a job and handle a boss." He referred particularly to his own continued schooling, which he explained as an attempt to avoid going out into the world, facing the job market, and settling down.

A man, married for fifteen years and unhappy with his job, defined self-confidence as the ability to "live without a paycheck." He wanted to quit his job and start his own business.

A thirty-three-year-old married woman described her quest for self-confidence as follows: "If I had self-confidence I wouldn't put up with my life for one minute longer. I'd go back to school and meet all sorts of new people. For me, self-confidence is the ability to meet people and feel you are as good as they are."

For the student, self-confidence involved holding a job, and for the husband, it meant the courage to give up a job. For the wife, self-confidence suggested the ability to meet new people. Of

15

course all three agree in a way, that self-confidence involves the personal courage or strength to change a situation. But every situation differs and, consequently, the means to reach each goal will also vary.

Behavior in a Situation

The quality of self-confidence, and all other such trait adjectives, are not characteristics that can be seen or located within a person. If we say that "Cindy has dark brown eyes," or that "Mary has a lovely smile," we are talking about appearances readily seen by all. But if we say, "Tony is extroverted," and we see Tony walking, sitting, reading, sleeping, or sunbathing, nothing about his physical being will enable us to confirm whether he really is outgoing. We need to see Tony with others, to judge whether or not he is actually extroverted. In fact, if we were given the assignment of verifying the rumor that Tony is extroverted, we would have to wait for the next party so we could watch him closely. Then, if Tony talks to a great many people, entertains with stories and anecdotes, and is sought after by all, we could agree that Tony is indeed extroverted. In contrast, if Tony were to sit quietly the whole evening, talking with only a single person, we would seriously doubt his reputed outgoingness. In short, our judgment of a personality characteristic is based on what happens in a situation. We recognize that people are not shy, extroverted, ambitious, argumentative, fearful, or confident in some internal, absolute, or unchanging way. We know that when we use words like these we are really describing *behavior in a situation*.

A critical step then in bringing about change within ourselves is to state what we want in terms of *behavior in a situation*. In other words, stop thinking of yourself as *being* "lazy" or "scared," or daydream about *being* "ambitious," "courageous," or whatever. We are not always lazy or never ambitious for these are not constant internal qualities. What we really mean when we say we are lazy is that in situations A, B, and C, we behave in ways identifiable as lazy. But under condition Y or in environment X, our actions are such that they could not in any way be called lazy. As a first step, therefore, we are required to describe the personality changes we want to produce as behavior in a situation. Liz, for example, had been told so often that she was cold, aloof, and distant that she came to believe it, "I want to be warm, " she complained, "But I don't have it in me. I'm not a warm person. I'd like to be, but it's not in me. I'm just a cold person inside, I guess."

Liz was instructed to discard all the notions she had about not being an innately warm person. She was informed that there is nothing inside her that is automatically affectionate or cool. She was shown, however, that certain behaviors in specific situations will be interpreted by others as signs of warmth. Liz was told to visualize a familiar situation in which her conduct would indicate warmth to others. This is what she came up with.

> Here's a situation I can see very clearly. I am working at my desk. I usually just ignore anybody else. Milly comes over and asks to use the calculator. I would usually not even look up. I'd normally not even say anything except maybe "Yeah" or grunt or something. Now what I could do is look up at her. She comes over and asks me and I look up at her and I smile. I say, "Sure, help yourself." I could even say something about the way she is dressed: "That's pretty," or "I like that, Milly, it looks good on you." Something like that.

The value of stating the changes we want to bring about in terms of behavior in a situation is twofold. First, it forces us to specify just exactly what it is we are after. Second, it gets us away from the sterile process of self-labeling. Like Liz most of us have all sorts of prejudices about our own character, particularly its supposed limitations and weaknesses. We think we possess traits such as laziness or procrastination, we stigmatize ourselves as cold and unloving or convince ourselves that we are anxious or puritanical. Here is an exchange between members of an encounter group in which a person believed that he, like so many of us, was inalterably shy. He just could not approach others, especially the opposite sex.

Barry: *I am shy. Period. I was born shy. I am shy now and I will always be shy. I have learned to live with that and that's all. But it makes me miserable.*

Celeste: *Well, how does this affect your relationships.*

Barry: *Well, I can't ever make an overture to a girl. It has to come from her. I just can't even ask her to have a cup of coffee with me. That's just how I am.*

Celeste: *You mean you can never start any kind of conversation or anything? Invite a girl even just for coffee or something?*

Barry: *No I can't do it. I am shy. I would like to but I can't even initiate anything with a woman. Not even a conversation. I just don't know how to start talking to them. I told you I am shy, just completely shy, inside and out. Inside-out shy.*

Celeste: *But you have talked to all of us here. You suggested last time we go over to the diner later. You're not shy here.*

Barry: *Well this is a different situation.*

If Barry is supposedly shy in all situations but not in the encounter group, he is not totally, irrevocably, and "inside-out" shy. Thus, the secondary value of describing our own habits, traits, and hang-ups as *behaviors in situations* enables us to see very clearly that what we are now is not unchangeable. You say you are lazy or inhibited. But it would be an easily won bet, human behavior being as varied as it is, that there is at least one situation (perhaps many) in which you are anything but lazy or inhibited. Hence, be sure not only to describe your plans for change in terms of behavior in a situation, but remember also that what you think you are is simply an accumulation of behaviors in situations. To be different, you will specify the new behaviors you want and the conditions under which they will occur.

Observe

In order to emphasize that we need to describe our personal goals in terms of behavior-in-a-situation, there is a step we have left out. That step is, *observe*. Before we can readily formulate what it is we want and the situations in which we want it to occur, we need first to find out what is actually happening. What are we actually doing? Have we labeled our current behavior correctly and is our consequent objective appropriate? Liz, for example, had long held the belief that she was cold, distant, and unloving. Yet she was never entirely sure that these adjectives actually described the way she felt. She knew that she socialized relatively little with others. She was aware too that, throughout her growing years, she had no really intimate friend. It seemed reasonable then, she supposed, to conclude that she was a very cold person, just as she had often been told by others. Still, everything did not fit into place. When Liz went to the movies she felt warmed by scenes of tenderness or affection. She was also very sentimental about her several younger nieces and nephews and enjoyed hearing about them. Was she justifiably called cold? Just what is her behavior?

There are many ways in which we can observe ourselves. We may, if we have a close and attentive friend, ask her or him to describe what they see us do in a specific situation. An alternative is to think back about everything we did today, yesterday, or during the weekend and carefully write down all of our feelings, actions, and behaviors. At first, we may not think we can recollect much, but as we sit down to write things out, the memories will come flowing back. One of the very best ways, however, to observe ourselves, to see what our behavior is like, is to imagine we are two persons.

Let your imagination divide you into two halves. One is acting out your usual part and the other half is standing aside, making note of everything that occurs. Deliberately double yourself and watch yourself as if you were witness to some enthralling drama. There is even a psychological term, *depersonalization*, for being both actor and audience simultaneously. Depersonalize, remove yourself from you, so that while the ordinary part of you acts out your usual role, the extraordinary part of you is the interested observer. Here is a young wife who had been told she was hostile. She had frequent battles with her husband just as she had stormy arguments throughout her adolescence. She did not feel hostility, hatred, or anger, yet she did seem to have far more than the ordinary number of fights with everyone she had ever been close to. What was happening? Was she really filled with rage (as one amateur psychologist friend kept telling her)?

> I had always been told I was hostile so I just came to believe it. But not entirely, because I really love Burt. But we argue so much. And it is my fault. So I could not pinpoint my trouble. So I started to watch. I had to find out what the trouble really was. What was happening that caused all the arguments? Was it my anger? It was very difficult for me to objectively watch at first. I would try to both be myself and, at the same time, try to remember what was happening. It

was easy when nothing much happened between Burt and me but when an argument started I would forget to be a watcher at the same time. But then as I practiced being objective it became a little easier. And then finally I saw what was happening. Most of the arguments started when Burt said something and right away I would disagree with him. Most of the time it was a very little thing he said. Like he would say, "It's too cold out to go swimming." And automatically I would say, "No, it's not!" So he would say that was ridiculous, that it was sixty-two degrees, and he knew I shivered at that temperature. So I would have to come back with something, such as that on that day I felt like swimming, and the argument would start. It would end up him saying I was bitchy and me telling him he was insensitive. But the point is I saw that the arguments always started when he said something and I automatically said "No." Whatever it was he said, even farfetched things I knew nothing about. I had just learned to reply to a conversation by disagreeing. Like he said one day as we got into the car, "It sure looks like we need new tires." I said, "It doesn't seem to me we do." So that argument started. He said, "Your mother really is a good cook." I answered, "She's just putting on a show, she's not so good." He said "It's not even October and it's already getting dark earlier." I disagreed. Just anything at all, I just saw myself automatically saying no, and another squabble would follow. I was not hostile at all. I just had the habit of saying no. That's all it was—just a bad habit. A dumb behavior.

By carefully observing herself and her situation, this woman was able to locate specifically what she needed to change. She wanted her relationship with her husband to be less argumentative and more peaceful. But without analyzing what was actually happening she could never have formulated her goals in terms of behavior in a situation.

What I want to do is, whenever my husband makes a statement, I will automatically say yes and agree. I can visualize us sitting down on Sunday morning and he is reading the paper and he says, "This administration is just squandering our money away," and I will feel a pull to disagree but instead I will say, "Yes I often get that impression too." Or he'll say, "*Without Bugles, Without Drums* is supposed to be a good movie. Let's go see it," and I will agree, "Yeah, sounds good."

Notice that when the wife observed her behavior she found a cause-effect sequence. Her disagreement, cause, had the effect of provoking an argument. As part of our observation, it is often useful to analyze what is happening as a cause-effect relationship. Sometimes we can even talk to ourselves to help us see what is actually going on.

Here is a salesman who described his goal as wanting to be aggressive. When he observed his interactions, however, and analyzed it as a cause-and-effect situation, a fairly different picture emerged.

> I watched myself very closely with Mr. Lucien. I was trying to sell him a big Olds and that is a costly item. We're now getting $7,900 for the basic car alone. That would be a nice commission. I kept thinking this to encourage myself, and he kept asking questions about our guarantee, repairs, mileage, and that. I noticed I would ignore his questions and I would tell him how great this car was. I would make up stuff about how many others I had sold. I told him I had all sorts of back orders and I couldn't spend that much time with him; we were so busy. I noticed I was hurrying him. I was pressuring him and I just ignored whatever he asked. And he had legitimate questions and I just did not have the answers to them because I really did not know the product.
>
> When you analyze then, the cause of my failure as a salesman is not that I lack aggressiveness. I am plenty aggressive. I do not listen, I am not informed, and I bully my customers. The effect is that I lose sales.

Notice that none of the people who observed themselves just stood back and congratulated themselves. They were not simply entertained by their antics. Instead, they carefully analyzed what they were doing and asked how they might change or improve the behaviors they saw. They observed themselves and later conducted a self-dialogue. They held a cross-examination, playing both the accused and the district attorney. Here is a mother who wanted to improve her relationship with her daughter. She is recalling an unhappy discussion of the daughter's supposed rebelliousness.

> Why did I accuse her of being sloppy? Well, she did leave her room a mess! Could it be that I was trying to show her I

was still boss? When she said that I did not respect her right
of privacy, was she pointing out that I took too many liber-
ties? Could it have been that I was jealous because she
seemed so happy when she got back from her father's place?
I did feel a sort of revenge when I told her she was sloppy.
She keeps accusing me of being bossy. Is it bossy to try to
enforce certain standards? Well, that may not be , but was it
right for me to throw that at her when she was telling me her
story and she seemed so happy? Maybe there is where it is.
She was bubbly, and in the middle I made this comment on
her being sloppy. She got mad. I felt a sense of triumph. I
had put her down. Why did I want to put her down? If it is
jealousy, what other situations would it have shown itself
in? How about bossiness? Could I be competing with her in
some way?

It is not necessary to include the entire cross-examination.
By the time the mother was finished with herself, she had examined several situations that resulted in difficulty with her child.
Ultimately she learned that her most frequent behavior was to
"put down" her daughter. Now that she understood what she did,
she could go on to specify the new behaviors she wanted.

Let's go back to Liz who had come to believe she was cold.
When she actually observed her interactions, it became quite
clear that the most likely adjective to describe her behavior was
introverted. Often as not, she was deeply involved in her own
thought processes and did not notice others. Or she preferred to
read or take a walk alone, rather than to socialize. But she did
like people and had many good affectionate feelings toward
friends and relatives. Yet she was not outgoing and not very expressive. By self-observation Liz was enabled to see that her behavior falsely communicated lack of concern and affection. With
just a few behavior changes, she could project warmth and still
lead the individualized life she desired.

Use A Model

But what if self-observation and examination do not result
in learning what to do in order to change? A college student
stated that she wanted to be more "popular." She carefully observed herself in many different situations, in class, at meetings,
at a friend's birthday party, and still did not know how to

specify the behaviors she herself wanted. She probed herself, wrote down her experiences, but continued to be at a loss as to what could be done. When this happens, study a model. Pick out someone who has the qualities you want. Use the observational powers you have sharpened on yourself, and focus on your model.

> I thought of someone who was popular and really nice so I picked Ginny as a model to study. She always has lots of friends, both sexes, and they're always glad to see her. She is involved in lots of activities and she is also very nice. Not conceited or superficial or like that. Here's what she does. She dresses well, but casually. She wears a lot of colors. She stands out, but not in a vulgar way. She smiles whenever anyone looks at her or talks to her. She always says other people's names. Like she just doesn't say, "Hi!"—she'll say "Hi, Marv." Or, when she talks to someone, she'll say their name a few times. She belongs to things and she goes there and talks up. I talked to two people who belong with her and they told me. Everything she does has the effect of making people notice her and they like her.

Again, in those instances when self-observation proves too difficult or is unproductive, study a model. Pick the person or persons that possess the quality you yourself want and study them carefully. What behaviors in what situations make them popular, peaceful, extroverted, warm, or self-confident? Which of their behaviors succeed? Which do not? Models cannot only tell you what to do, they can also let you know the behaviors to avoid.

> Selwyn is a salesman with as poor a track record as mine. I watched him and it really drove the point home. He ignored every question his customers asked. He insulted them by saying they didn't know enough about the machinery to make judgments. He told them he was giving them a special deal because he liked them, and everyone there knew that was about as bald a lie as you could tell. Most of these things I watched, I do myself.

Studying a model is very useful, but be warned, do not rely upon your model's self-description. Persons who have the behaviors you want are not guaranteed to be knowledgeable about themselves. The college student who studied Ginny in order to understand why Ginny was popular subsequently talked to Ginny.

> When I got to know her better, I asked her about her being popular. She said she knew she had a lot of friends and said it was because she had a high standard of self-respect. She said her mother always taught her that, if she never did anything she was ashamed of, other people would sense that she could be proud of herself. She advised me to live so I could respect myself, and then others would come to me. I would be admired by others. The amazing thing is that she doesn't really understand that she is friendly, well dressed, and does all the things that make people like her. It has nothing to do with self-respect. She is popular because of her behavior.

Here lies one of the reasons why so many people fail to achieve their own goals. They want to be ambitious like Jed, or popular like Ginny, or sexy like Lourdis, or relaxed like Mark, and they ask these persons for their secret. What they come away with is more than likely the inaccurate result of faulty insight. Instead of good useful information, they are given an erroneous collection of clichés and misunderstood behaviors. Do *not* interview your models, but observe them. Do not be guided by what your models say, but by what they do. It may turn out that they are not really popular or relaxed as you thought they were. You will only learn this from careful observation. But if they demonstrate the qualities you want, you will have learned something that can help you start your own process of change.

Targeting Your Behavior

Now that you have learned to observe and concretely describe, it is time to focus on your own behavior. What characteristics do you want to be rid of, keep, or increase? To find your own behavioral target, begin by thinking of a time or incident in which your conduct displeased you. Don, for example, is a musician and is very unhappy about what he calls his laziness. In order to specify the behavior he wants to change, he has to provide an illustration of his supposed laziness.

> We hadn't worked since February and this guy calls me up from Woodstock and we could have a gig Saturday night. Now everybody is restless. The drummer is going to the city.

We're going to lose Lenny and his guitar, you know. So if I can pull this group together on Saturday it'll mean we stay together a little longer. We could probably play in Woodstock for a few months, I think. But I just couldn't get myself to get them all together. You know the phone calls, and your calling information, or this guy's living with his aunt. Just too much hassle. That's an example of when my laziness just kills me. I mean the whole group is just falling apart and I'm too lazy to try to hold them together.

Neville wants to worry less. He considers himself an "anxiety neurotic." In order for him to change, he too must begin by recalling an instance when he worried too much.

An example of when I was very displeased with my behavior was when my doctor told me he wanted me to get my kidneys X-rayed. They were going to inject a dye and take pictures. I had gone to him because of this urinary thing. Anyway he said he did not expect to find anything but it was just routine. A precaution he said. Those words stuck in my mind. A precaution against what? The more I thought about it, the more worried I got. I had an appointment for the X-ray in a few days and then it would be more than a week till I went back to my doctor to get the results. So I had about ten days to build up worrying about it. Each day got worse. First I thought, well, maybe they'll find something like an infection and I'll just get some more antibiotics. Then I kept seeing things in the newspapers about kidney machines, and I saw a TV show about dialysis. It's painful and costly. So every day I worried more and more about what they would find and what I would have to put up with. Maybe I would die. What happened actually is that my appetite got worse and worse. I woke up in the morning feeling nauseous. I gave up eating breakfast. I slept badly. I had nightmares about being in a machine for the rest of my life. I had periods during the day when my heart would race and pound. I sweated. My hands were cold. I lost about seven pounds. It's unbelievable, isn't it? Of course, when I went back to the doctor, there was nothing wrong with my kidneys. Just as he said, it was just routine. He just wanted to have those X-rays for my record. I want to stop getting so upset over nothing. I want to stop my mind from visualizing just the worst possibilities.

After recalling a situation in which you disliked yourself, extract from it the behavior that you want to change. The musician,

Don, wants to respond immediately to requests and responsibilities. He wants to be able to make phone calls when they are needed. Neville wants to be able to go to the doctor and not experience the palpitating heart, nausea, clammy perspiration, and other indications of anxiety. Both men have used one of their typical unhappy life experiences to dissect out the behavior they want to modify. This is generally a good way to isolate targets. First, recall the behavior in a situation that displeases and zero in on the exact behaviors you want to alter. Second, say to yourself what it is you want to be able to do. Imagine or visualize a scene demonstrating your target behavior. For Don, the second step, imagining the desired behavior, was described this way:

> I give Lenny a call. I try his old number. There is no answer.
> I knew that. I call information. She gives me his new
> number. It is nine in the morning so I know he will be home.
> I call him and he answers and that makes me feel good.

Paul says he is afraid of women. In order to target his behavior as a first step, he recalls being in a bar with a male friend and both were completely unable to approach any of the single women. They hung back, feeling frightened, awkward, and out of place.

> I have to explain that I grew up in a very devout family.
> Until I was a teenager, everyone including myself, thought I
> would be a priest. When I was fourteen, my mother died
> and we were raised by my oldest sister. She was twenty-four
> and not married. And she was the only girl and there were
> four of us boys. So we began to raise a lot of hell. My father
> wasn't very concerned about us.
>
> Anyway my mother's memory remained with me. She
> had always talked about my being a priest. She had made
> me very fearful of God. There were a lot of things you could
> do or think about that were a sin. And she kept me from
> them. Then when she died, we did pretty much as we
> pleased. And I started feeling, at the same time, that what
> we were doing was a sin. After a while, practically everything was a sin.
>
> Anyway, in this bar, I was just paralyzed. Some girl
> would look at me and my heart would pound and I would
> turn away. I would make believe I did not see her. My friend
> kept saying, "Go over, talk to her," but I couldn't. There

were a lot there. It's a singles place. That's why I was practically paralyzed in that bar. And I always am with women.
I'm afraid. I can't get near them before I freak out.

Now if you want me to turn that around into my goal,
to imagine that second step, here's how I see it. Peter and I
are in the bar. We see these two girls, gorgeous and blah,
blah. We invite them for a drink to come over to our booth.
We talk to them. We all laugh a lot. We leave pretty late
and I have my arm around the one with long black hair. We
go to their place and we make love all night long.

Paul did well with his first step, describing the behavior in its
context of the wish to change. But when he took the second step
imagining a favorable situational outcome, he was much too
grandiose. Paul is pathologically afraid of women. His target
cannot start out by being the flawless seduction of his fantasied
dark-haired beauty. Our behavioral targets must be small attainable goals. As each reasonable objective is reached, then we can
go on to the next.

The purpose of recalling a real-life example of our conduct
that makes us unhappy is to spot, to pinpoint, the exact behavior we want to change. This enables us to visualize our first,
modest behavioral target. Don's objective is to be able to tele-
phone his friends. Paul's objective should be to learn to smile at,
perhaps even say a word or two to strange women in a bar. That
is a fair start for he has a long, long way to go before he can be at
ease with the opposite sex.

When we begin the process of change, we will continuously
recollect real-life situations that made us unhappy. We will recall
how we handled situations in the past and specify how we would
like to behave in similar situations in the future. And our targets
should always be only a very few steps away. Paul will not be able
to have complete relationships with women for quite some time.
And Neville, the man overly concerned about his kidney X-ray
will have to work very slowly and gradually to reduce all his anxiety symptoms and the many situations that initiate them. When
we think about changing our personalities and our lives, it is well
to recall the ancient proverb: the journey of a thousand miles
begins with a single step.

Keep A Record

When you have targeted your behavior, that is, when you know precisely what it is you want to change, start keeping a record. This record will enable you to see your progress or warn you if you are faltering. To keep a record, use some graph paper or improvise something similar. Look at Figure 1. This is a typical record. Along the base line are the days of the month. The vertical, or side axis, shows the target behavior. In Figure 1, it is the number of "agreement" responses made by the wife who was generally very negativistic towards her husband, children, and friends. Notice that the April record is before any attempts were made to modify behavior. The program for change began May 1.

There are several important points in recording your behavior. First, there must always be a record of a month or more of your original, unchanged behavior. This is needed as a sample to provide contrast. It will enable you to judge whether you are actually making progress. Notice, for instance, that the person in Figure 2 does not seem to be bringing about any noticeable change in his behavior. This graph alerts him to carefully reconsider what he is doing.

The base line of the chart is always an indication of time. Usually it is convenient to keep a daily record. Sometimes, however, behavior will be fairly infrequent so that the base line will be weekly. In Figure 3, Paul added up the total number of "eligible" women with whom he had even a slight conversation during the previous week. Notice that during the first week of April Paul talked to only one woman. In the third week of April he talked to three but during the last week he talked only to one again. After he started on his program of self-change, his record of conversation in May increased steadily.

Sometimes a simple count of the number of times the target behavior occurs (or does not occur) is not very revealing. For Neville, for example, it was far more revealing for him to count how many minutes of anxiety he experienced every day, than the total number of incidents. He tended to have only one or two things a day that made him fearful. In order for him to see if his fear behavior was decreasing, he needed to record how long each episode lasted. In Figure 4, it can be seen that during April, before behavior change, he had anxiety episodes most days and

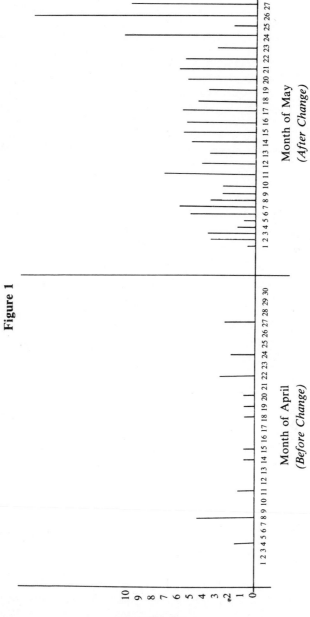

Figure 1

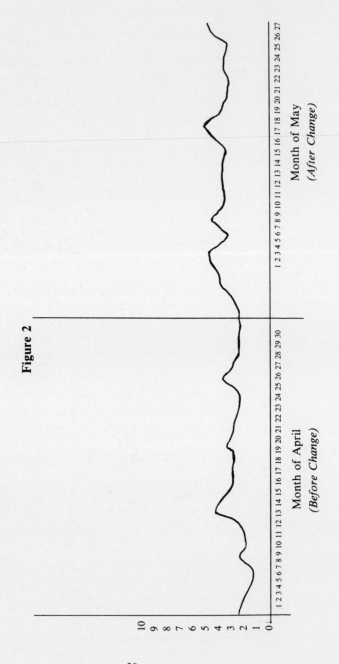

Figure 2

Month of April
(Before Change)

Month of May
(After Change)

30

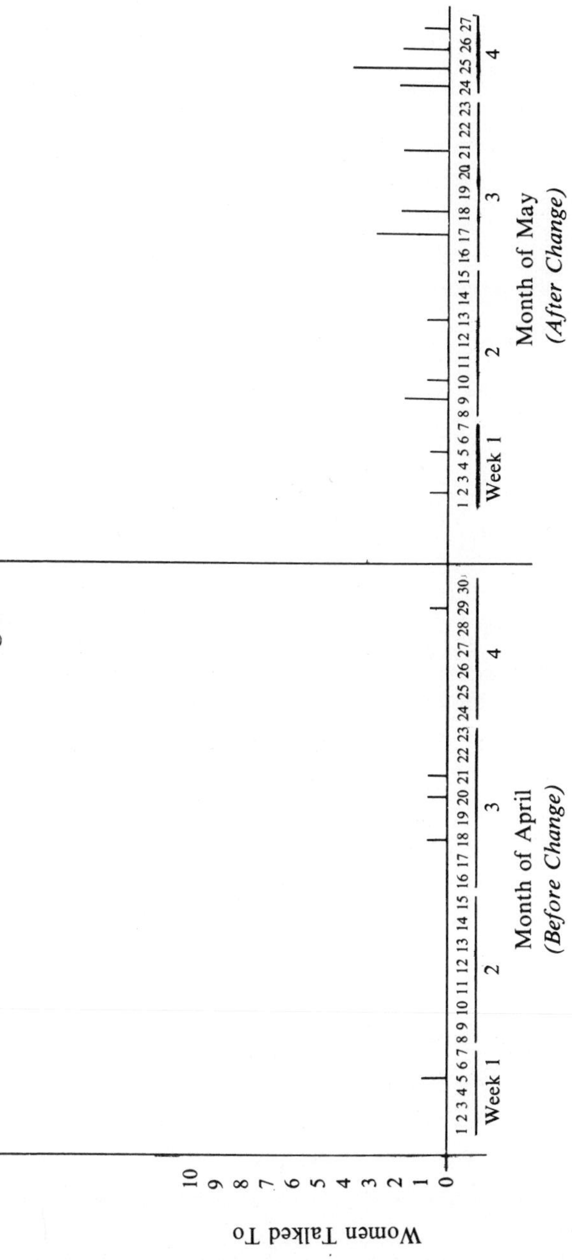

Figure 3

31

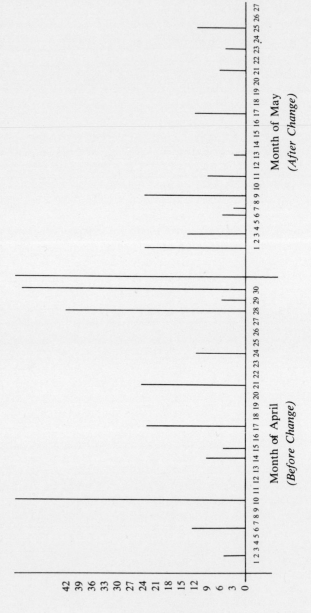

Figure 4

Minutes of Anxiety

Month of April
(Before Change)

Month of May
(After Change)

32

they lasted from three to four minutes to well over an hour. In May, following behavior change, the length of attacks slowly but steadily decreased.

The records illustrated cover each of two months, before and after self-change efforts. But many personality-change programs last a long time or occur very, very slowly. Sometimes, as a result, a record of behavior both before and after change may be many months long. In other words, keep a record for as long as you need to continue to work on your personality change, whether it be a week or a year. Do not be discouraged if there are occasional setbacks. Progress is never totally smooth.

The figures shown above and the various alternatives cited by no means exhaust all the possible ways in which you can record your own behavior. There are very many techniques you can use to visualize your efforts. Some people are, in fact, very creative, using interesting materials, crayons, or three-dimensional representations to chart their personality change. It does not really matter, however, whether your records are highly original or very ordinary as long as you find a suitable method of indicating what you're doing and stick with it. The important thing is that it give a clear, direct picture of your progress.

Three
Why—
Willpower
and
Motivation

Florence had six stormy years of married life with her husband. She was determined either to try to make her marriage more peaceful or end it once and for all. Thinking about the many tensions and arguments she had, she recognized that, if she were a more alert and conscientious person, her marriage would improve greatly. Many of the fights she had with her husband seemed to center about her apparent forgetfulness and disorganizaton.

It's a lot of little things that add up. Here's what I did last week. I mean anyone of them alone is petty. But, you know, coming one after the other as they always do, they drove my husband crazy. On Sunday, we couldn't find his car keys. I had taken them off the dresser that morning and driven to get the paper. We searched high and low. I guess I put them on the seat of the car after I parked and they had slipped into the crack between the cushions. It took hours to find them. We had a terrible fight about that. On Monday I was supposed to pick up his suit so he could wear it for the interview on Tuesday morning. Naturally I forgot. He made me call up the cleaner at 9 that night, at home, and open up his store. That fight was awful too. On Wednesday I couldn't find the checkbook. On Friday I did two things. I invited Joanne and her husband to dinner and play bridge that night. I knew he can't stand them but I figured, "Oh, so what!" But the other boner was even better. I was out all day Friday so I had put a roast in the oven on "Time Bake." But I didn't set the clocks correctly. So, here we both come home around 7:30 and the roast, potatoes, and everything are just stone cold. And here Joanne is coming in half an hour.

I know these things might sound silly to other couples, but they're serious for us. I mean he starts calling me names, he yells, I cry. It becomes hysterical. I could go on and on. I just have to be able to get control of my time, to just remember better and just make things work so we can stop fighting.

Although friends were often amused by Florence, she herself was very unhapppy. She resolved therefore to work out a careful step-by-step plan to help her organize her day, to remember, and to be alert.

This book, that I mentioned, was my guide. For example, I wrote down every responsibility for that day, as it recommended. I would follow the list carefully. But then half of the time I would lose the list. I love just to sit with my feet up, drink some coffee, and read a story. So I was supposed to reward myself with that on any day that I reached three o'clock without screwing up. Well, thinking about my reward was so appealing that I started staying in, reading, the first thing in the morning. Before you knew it I'd blown most of the day just lolling around, reading, drinking coffee, and that. It just didn't work. I guess because I just didn't have the willpower. Maybe that's what I really lack is willpower.

Willpower

Is Florence correct in saying that her failure to change is due to a lack of willpower? She had, after all, learned some perfectly good techniques which could have helped her modify her personality. She knew what to do but just did not do it. She herself put it, "I'm just not lucky enough to be one of those persons born with a lot of willpower."

Most people, like Florence, think of willpower as some sort of native aptitude such as, for example, musical talent. We all know of an occasional individual that barely ever had a lesson yet seems to be remarkably musical. These persons can remember any tune or easily pick out a melody on a piano or guitar. In contrast, the rest of us are usually so ungifted that it is difficult for us to learn to play even one instrument. But willpower is not like musical potential. Willpower is not given in greater or lesser amounts to different people when they are born. None of us has inherently high or low, good or poor willpower.

When we complain of trouble with our willpower, we are really talking about low or conflicting motivation. Thus when Florence failed to carry out her carefully planned behaviors, we should immediately examine her motives. Why is she not applying herself? Could it be she is not really motivated to be reconciled with her husband? Instead of just shrugging off her failure as a lack of willpower, we should inquire into the reasons behind her continued negligence.

It is instructive to peek in on Florence's first therapy session. After a particularly bitter fight, Florence had taken her daughter and moved out. Very quickly however, she felt alone, discouraged, and helpless, and sought professional counseling. She told her therapist that before separating, she had mastered a number of learning techniques that would have enabled her to plan ahead, remember, and organize her time and activities. Yet somehow, in one way or another, she seemed to be sabotaging what she was supposed to be doing. She herself was beginning to suspect there was a reason, a motive, behind all her actions. But she needed first to clear up her thinking concerning her supposed poor willpower.

Florence: *I think, that is I don't really know, but could it be my low willpower? I mean I just don't have much.*

Therapist: *You believe that some people just have very little willpower. You feel you have only a little willpower so there's not much you can do about it.*

Florence: *Well. Yes! It's not my fault that I failed. Right? I just don't have much willpower.*

Therapist: *Your argument is this: (1) It's not my fault, I wasn't given much willpower; (2) You need willpower to change; (3) I couldn't change because of low willpower. Therefore, (4), it's not my fault I couldn't change.*

Florence: *(laughs). Right. It's not my fault. Seriously, I couldn't change. I just did not have enough willpower.*

Therapist: *O.K. Let's be accurate and translate willpower into motivation. Then we can get someplace. You see everyone has motivation. If their motivation is in harmony with their*

*objectives, they have what you would call high willpower. In
your case, it looks very much as if your motives to change are
in conflict. Part of you wants to change, to have peace with
your husband. But maybe part of you does not. So what you
call low willpower may really be a case of powerful motives* not
change, coming into conflict with motives to change.

Later in the first therapy session, Florence began to agree
that perhaps there might have been some motives that were impelling her *not* to change. Despite the fact that she believed and
said she wanted to be more thoughtful and efficient, there
might be reasons why she did not want to be more alert. Her
reluctance'to pursue her program of behavior change might
not be due to low willpower but actually the result of her
hidden need to remain as she was.

> I think I love my husband, you know. I guess I really do
> want a good marriage. . .I mean maybe sometimes I might
> resent him. Maybe even my marriage. I mean I might have
> thought here and again how maybe, what it would be like if
> I were free. I think that's common. A lot of people think
> that. It doesn't mean anything. Do you think that maybe I
> wasn't really trying because I did not want to? I mean you
> don't think, do you, that I was really motivated not to
> change, because I wanted my marriage to fail, or something.
> Do you?

Whenever we say we lack the willpower to do A, B, or C,
what we really mean is that we are not *motivated* to do A, B, or
C. What we should understand however, is that all our actions
are motivated. If we are *not* motivated to be reconciled with our
husbands, then maybe we are motivated to break up. If we are
not motivated to drink less, or be affectionate, then we may be
motivated to do the opposite. For every behavior there is a
motive just as for every effect there is a cause.

Sigmund Freud, more than any other psychologist, pointed
out that underlying every action, every behavior, every response,
there is a motive. Nothing we do or say is accidental. In fact,
Freud demonstrated it is the supposedly accidental act, the slip of
the tongue, the forgetful behavior, that is actually most revealing
of our true motives. When she sought professional help, Florence
described at some length her feelings about her husband. She
seemed, however, to continue to stumble over certain words. Her

verbal slips revealed a good deal more about Florence's real feelings than she intended.

> Of course I like my husband. No, I mean I don't like him. No, I am trying to say I don't just like him. I don't love him but I don't like him. No! No! This is crazy! I'm getting so mixed up. I'll say it right. I know I can. I like him. More than that. I do not just like him. I love him. I really do. There! I said it right.

What some of us call a slip of the tongue or a mistake, Freud showed was really the "unconscious talking." Many of our desires are hidden even from ourselves. But when we are tired, sleeping, off guard, preoccupied, when our alertness slips, our unconscious has an opportunity to reveal itself.

Motives—Conscious and Unconscious

We are not aware of all our motives. There are a great many needs that are hidden by our own rationalizations and defenses. Florence, the seemingly careless wife, was convinced that she really wanted to better her relationship with her husband. "I really and truly want to become an organized and more careful person. I really, really deep down want to have a better life together." Nevertheless, despite her protestations of motivation Florence finally learned that her true motives were essentially opposite to those on the surface. In order to reach our behavioral objectives, to change our personality, we must learn to become as aware as possible of all our motives, conscious and unconscious.

Freud pointed out that our motivation is like an iceberg. The motives that are obvious, on the surface, are but a small part of the whole. Most drives lie below the surface; they are unconscious. In a sense *unconscious* is an unfortunate word: it sounds like a part of the brain in which all sorts of unknown needs are tucked away. But there is really nothing at all mysterious about unconscious motives or memories. These are simply needs and experiences of which we are not immediately aware. After all, we cannot be tuned in to our every emotion and perception. There is much too much taking place all the time to understand and focus clearly on every sensation.

In addition to the fact that *the unconscious* is a reservoir of what we might call simply unrecognized wishes and memories, it also contains feelings deliberately pushed out of consciousness. Some of our desires or our past may be unacceptable to us. Perhaps we had a dreadful experience as a child. Such a happening could be much too disturbing for us to want to remember so we push it out of awareness. Or we have some negative emotion toward our mother, child or spouse, and these feelings of rage or hatred make us feel painfully guilty. So, to avoid this discomfort, we push these attitudes out of consciousness. The process of forcing disturbing feelings away from our awareness is called repression. We deliberately, in secret even from ourselves, remove from our awareness all memories, experiences, and motives that will in one way or another make us seriously uncomfortable.

But, the critical point about unconscious motivation is that though we do not recognize or recall our hidden feelings, *they still remain powerful energizers of our actions*. We have already seen them operating in Florence's case. She was truthfully not aware of her deep dislike of her marriage and her ambition to end it. Nevertheless these potent drives continued to influence her conduct. On the surface she hoped to be an adequate person. But underneath, her motivation to end the marriage succeeded in disrupting every conscious move she made to improve.

Because of the strength of unconscious motives, it is most important that we examine ourselves thoroughly when our plans for change do not seem to work. The worst thing we can do is to blame our willpower. Putting the blame on willpower is a rationalization, an excuse not to look further and find the real cause of our failure. When we are unable to carry out our behaviors or reach our goal, willpower has nothing to do with it. In fact, it is time to recognize that willpower is a fiction. For our purposes there is *no such thing as willpower*. There is only motivation, conscious and unconscious. When plans fail, search out the unconscious needs, drives and attitudes that are blocking progress.

There are a number of ways we ourselves can examine our motives and reach into our unconscious. In the following, two such techniques, *attention* and *dreams*, will be discussed. But the exploration of ourselves, the aware and unaware, is a difficult task. It is likely the most challenging part of personality change. It is often advisable, therefore, to work with a close friend who can serve as a sort of reality check on our self-analysis. We can teach our friend what we know about analyzing dreams, for example, and ask him for his interpretation. Often the results of such a dialogue are more rewarding than examining our own hidden motives alone.

Attend

An anecdote from the Zen literature tells of the student who went to a Zen master and asked for the word conveying the highest wisdom. The Zen master turned to the student and immediately spoke the word, "Attention." The student was confused and asked the master to say more. The master spoke again and said, "Attention. Attention." The young man was irritated and demanded finally that the master at least define his words. At this the master answered, "Attention means attention."

Zen argues that the highest wisdom is attention. The ancient Greeks said "Know thyself." Both suggest the attentive probing of ourselves and our life. In contrast, most of us attend very little to our existence or what is happening around us. Our life has become a habit. We are so conditioned by our daily routine that without much thought we do our work, meet obligations and almost mechanically pursue our pleasures. Often what we believe to be careful personal choices or decisions are simply unimaginative exercises in habit. Since our lives are so unoriginal, so repetitive and unvaried, how can we break through, obtain insight and attend?

We can know ourselves, we can attend by attending to each old and familiar routine as if it were brand new. Let each personal experience be fresh. Start from the beginning or at least make believe you are. Here is an example provided by a man who had been trying very unsuccessfully to overcome his severe fear of all doctors and most particularly dentists.

Ed was twenty-seven-years-old, single and of average appearance except for his noticeably bad teeth. Not only were his teeth crooked but they were visibly stained, in need of cleaning and repair. The effect of his poor dental hygiene was that as soon as Ed began to talk he looked homely and unkempt. To correct this situation, Ed had begun a behavior desensitization program to overcome his fear of dentists. This was actually Ed's third attempt to overcome his dental phobia and like his others, this too was failing. He was not keeping to his practice schedule, somehow seemed to forget instructions, and appeared to be subverting his own progress. Of course, Ed was eager to excuse himself by blaming his "willpower," but the therapist he was working with did not permit this rationalization. Instead, he informed Ed that perhaps there were some unconscious motives that might be impelling him to maintain his fear of dentists and keep his teeth in disrepair. Ed was assigned to watch himself very closely. He picked Sunday afternoon, a relatively relaxed time, to start attending. He would treat that entire period as if it were a brand new experience.

> I watched myself like crazy all afternoon. But nothing. . .paying attention like it was brand new. . .but the same old thing, just playing tennis. Then, this was routine too, Gordie picked up these two girls playing tennis. Nice! I'm not too good with women but he's doing all the work so here's a chance for me. I really attend. Now let's see what's actually happening. . .I watch myself, then, everything. We're talking. He likes the darker one. I start talking to the other one. She's turning off. It's my mouth. Who can blame her? She says to herself, "He's gross," or something like that. Anyway, watch what's happening! I feel bad. Of course I feel bad! Then I catch this something else. Another feeling I have. I think it is relief. Just this little feeling of relief. It only seems to last one thousandth of a second. But my attention caught it. But I also feel bad. That lasts. It's not going to go anywhere and I feel bad. But I caught this split second feeling that it is good too.

By attending to his feelings very closely, Ed found an entirely new dimension of his experience. He was not afraid of women and he did not have any sexual phobia, as such. He had several relationships but they were always very casual. In all his intimacies, the situation or the woman made it obvious that the relationship was purely sexual and very limited. But when Ed approached an interaction that might become substantial, he was fearful. He did not want to be "trapped, tied down and domesticated," as he put it. Thus, beginning with his recognition of the momentary feeling of relief when the girl was repelled by his teeth, he was able to ferret out his entire complex of unconscious motives. He wanted to keep his ugly teeth. They helped him scare off "nice" or "eligible" girls. He had to remain afraid of dentists so he would have an excuse not to have his teeth repaired. His unhygienic teeth were his defense against what he thought of as domestic entrapment. On the surface, he was motivated to have his teeth repaired, but underneath, unconsciously, he was powerfully driven to keep his teeth and everything just the way they were.

For most of our existence, our attention is scattered. We mix in all sorts of sights, sounds, feelings and experiences. We do not separate out our own reactions, our own momentary perceptions and responses. But in order to reach into our unconscious, we need to focus more clearly. We need to have all our antennae out, to attend as fully as we can to what is actually happening. We have to catch those tiny subtle feelings and responses that last only a fraction of a second. We have to hold on to thoughts and emotions that fade in and out so swiftly that without the most careful attention they would entirely escape our notice. When we have caught some of these experiences, then the process of unravelling our unconscious can begin.

Dreams

Freud said dreams were the royal road to the unconscious. There is little doubt that dreams provide the surest path to our inner selves. What we hide so well when we are awake comes fully into the open when our guard is down, when we are asleep. But dreams are not without their deceptions either. Freud distinguished what he called the manifest from the latent content. The manifest content of the dream is the apparent story or event. The latent content is the hidden meaning. We need to analyze the dream, understand its symbols and substitutions.

Let us return to Florence, the supposedly inefficient wife. We already suspect her failure to become organized was unconsciously motivated. During her third therapy session, she related the following dream:

> I had this very short dream, just this morning before waking up, I think. But it stuck in my mind. It is very vivid. I

was buying something in a store. Macy's I think. This
woman, the cashier, she was very nice to me. Then there was
this young boy who looked like this kid I knew in high
school. He asked the cashier for some boiling water. To me
this was an innocent and a beautiful thing to request. But
she, the cashier, she got mad at him. She took out what
could be a rifle, I think. She started yelling at me and him.
She was yelling something like "I don't have hot water!" I
think I ran outside with the boy. I said something like come
to my house, you can take a hot shower there. I gave him
directions and I think I was glad it all happened, something
like that. I woke up, I think, as he was coming to my house.
I had the shower running. I could hear it as I woke up.

Through the careful interpretation of this dream (and subsequently others), it became clear that Florence's real motive was
not reconciliation with her husband. She did not really want to
learn to live harmoniously with her spouse but instead wanted to
live without him. In this dream the young boy made her recall
how attached she had been to a high school boy friend who
wanted to marry her. But his father was a career serviceman and
had moved his family, and her boy friend, twelve thousand miles
away during her third year of high school. She had several other
aborted love affairs in college and in her sophomore year married
her husband more out of frustration than love. Florence suggested also that the clerk's anger at the young boy reminded her
of her own mother's anger at some of the suitors she herself had.
Her mother always seemed displeased at the boy friends she liked
best. In a way, however, she was pleased at her own mother's disapproval. For the more she disapproved, the more Florence
enjoyed "taking them home for a shower," the symbolism of
which is obvious.

To assist you in understanding your own dreams, follow
these instructions. First, always jot down immediately, whether
in the middle of the night or when you wake up in the morning,
the entire dream. Omit nothing! Keep a pad and pencil handy by
your bed so that you can keep an immediate record. Dreams are
quickly forgotten unless you have notes that serve as a reminder.

Second, look for the hidden meaning of the dream. Do not
accept the manifest content as a statement of your motivation.
Dreams are a disguised expression of what we really want or

secretly fear. In your mind turn the dream over, dissect and re-construct it to find the hidden meaning. Freud pointed out that behind every dream, a real story waits to be told.

A good way for finding the inside meaning of our dreams is (like Florence) to ask ourselves what the different elements in the dream remind us of. What did this character or situation suggest? Who or what does this person or event resemble? What was there about this circumstance that seems so familiar? Let your mind wander freely and it will guide your interpretation.

Ed, with the bad teeth, had a dream that revealed just how fearful he was of being trapped. He related a long, complicated dream about being on an island, chased by cannibals and falling into a large hole. While the pursuers danced around the hole, he felt strangely at ease in his captivity. Oddest of all, the hole had posters on the wall.

> The posters really get me. They reminded me of my room at home. That's it. I was trapped again, like at home. And those cannibals—they wore skirts, they were women. That's it. That's my fear right there. It was a nightmare! I'm going to end up trapped just like when I was a kid. Wait. These cannibals—these women—they were wearing necklaces made out of teeth. Wow! That's it. They had made me go and lose my teeth. They had them, my teeth, and then they had caught me. Wow. It's all there.

A third instruction in interpreting our own dreams is to look for symbols. Very often wishes, fears, even entire events and sit-uations are symbolized by a relatively simple-seeming object. A middle-aged man who was trying to be more independent both at home and on his job was having great difficulty in reaching his goal. He seemed to be unconsciously motivated not to be inde-pendent. He told the following dream:

> I'm flying. I think in Montana. We're going to shoot eagles from the plane. I read about that a while ago. I don't re-member a lot but I think I had an argument with the pilot. Anyway I dive out of the plane. No parachute. I just dive out. I glide down and down. It feels good. I like it. I just glide into an eagle's nest. Then an eagle flies to me. I'm not scared. He's bringing me two oranges. I wake up and I think this is crazy but I feel good.

To detect the meaning of symbols, we need once again to ask ourselves what does this or that symbol bring to mind. We need to let our thoughts roam freely. We have to uninhibit our thinking so that even the most foolish-seeming association is not passed up.

> You know when I think about the symbols of this dream, the oranges keep popping back into my head. I let my mind wander. Oranges. Oranges. The one thought I had and I don't know that it makes sense, is that they are breasts. O.K., they are breasts! Wait. Hold it. That's it. It's my mother. She was a full-bosomed woman. She was so nice to me. When I was home from college, she would bring me orange juice in bed. To get started. Then she would fuss over me—I see it. The oranges are a symbol for my mother and how she took care of me. It all fits in. I'm back in the nest, being taken care of. I don't want to be independent. I want to be taken care of again, like a little boy.

Dreams are the royal road to the unconscious, though analysis requires patience and persistence. But learning to understand them is also a pleasurable exercise in imagination and creativity. Additional help, when necessary, is available in Sigmund Freud's excellent book, *The Interpretation of Dreams*, found in most libraries and bookstores.

In addition to the means presented so far to understand our unconscious motives, there are several others. Some may try fantasy, letting their mind and imagination wander to see what thoughts and insights occur spontaneously. Others may have success with forms of meditation, similar to fantasy. Just focus on a specific problem and meditate upon it. Often, solutions occur that originate in the unconscious. Still another technique for probing our hidden feelings is to cross-examine ourselves. Hold a self-dialogue, asking yourself why you do this or did that. Typically, these introspective self-examinations are far more thorough than any interrogation by someone else. In all these ways we frequently ferret out the secret motivations that may have a powerful, yet unrecognized effect on our behavior.

Conclusion

We have learned that whenever we have difficulty progressing toward our behavioral goal, the chances are very good that unconscious motives are blocking our path. Florence could not become more organized, or Ed repair his teeth, because both were secretly driven in the opposite direction. As long as they were unaware of the real source of their lack of progress there was little they could do. At best, they could excuse their poor performance by blaming it on low willpower, a rationalization we now recognize as thoroughly invalid.

We cannot deal with motives that block our path when these motives remain unconscious. That is why we need to diligently pursue the reasons behind any failure to change our personality, to discover our unconscious. When our motives become known we can handle them and plan with intelligence and reason. After she became aware of her unconscious need to be free of her husband, Florence said:

> As long as I didn't know why, I couldn't straighten out. I was confused and unhappy. When I finally learned it was because I really did not want to live with him anymore, then I could deal with it. You know. Then I could make some sane decisions, you know. You can't make any decisions when you don't know what you really want. When you know, you can decide.

Similarly, as Ed learned that he deliberately kept his teeth in bad shape to ward off girl friends, he was for the first time able to manage his phobia of dental work.

> I'm still not at ease with women. Particularly if I suspect it could be serious. I still don't want to marry, let's face it. I like my freedom. But I know now it's silly to use ugly teeth to keep them away. I can avoid them getting serious in lots of other ways. So, I removed that block anyway, and I'm actually seeing a dentist now, for the first time in twelve years, since I was a kid and my mother made me go.

After we recognize formerly hidden motives, we can usually resume work toward our behavioral goal. But in many instances when buried feelings are uncovered, our objective may have to change. Florence, for example, had to deal with conflicting drives. She wanted to preserve her marriage but she also wanted her freedom again. Ultimately, her need to be independent was the stronger and her goal was thus changed to learning behaviors that would enable her to return to school, study, and live confidently on her own.

When motives that were once unconscious come to the surface, they may conflict with conscious desires. Outwardly, we might be impelled towards goal A but inwardly our urges are for goal B. Or the same goal may both attract and repel us. This was true for Ed who wanted on the surface to have his teeth fixed but was also secretly driven to keep them unattractive. Once we discover our hidden motives only to find conflict, the next question is, how do we resolve disagreement? Working out conflicting motivations is the subject of the next chapter.

Four
Solving
Conflict

This chapter is a sequel to Chapter Three on willpower and motivation. The preceeding section suggested that when our plans to change fail, it is often the result of hidden opposing motivation. The means to uncover such unconscious opposition were presented. In this section, the ways to resolve conflict, to untangle ambivalent needs, are explained.

The methods described to straighten out conflicting feelings will prove of help for two kinds of persons. First, they are for those who, newly conscious of conflicting motivation, want to settle their dilemmas and change their personality. Second, these methods are also for people for whom indecisiveness is the central problem. There are quite a few people who are not unconsciously in conflict but do have chronic difficulty making any kind of choice. The only personality change they want, or need, is to learn how to solve their continual ambivalence and finally move ahead towards a specific goal.

Types of Conflict

Conflict is an everyday experience. It may be minor as when we are confronted with the problem of which pair of shoes to buy. The dark brown ones are just the style we have been looking for but they are slightly uncomfortable. The comfortable and good-looking ones, however, are extremely expensive. What to do? Sometimes our conflicts are much more serious. Marriage (or divorce) has been proposed to us. There are lots of sound reasons to go ahead but we are also motivated to hold back. We are in the uncomfortable position of knowing that, whatever our choice, we may well regret it. Likely as not, the end result is that we do neither. We walk out of the store without shoes and we do not marry (or divorce) simply because we cannot make up our mind.

Much of our behavior, both trivial and significant, results from a mixture of feelings. There are few decisions we make or goals that we pursue that are simple, straightforward and totally free of conflict. Since much of our conduct is accompanied by ambivalence it should not surprise us that our plans for personality change may also be somewhat conflicted. We think we want to be more assertive, outspoken, and candid, but when we really examine all of our motivation, we are not so sure. Or we think we want to reduce our fear of tests so that we can go back to school but as soon as we get started on a desensitization program, we always seem to get sidetracked.

Many of our conflicts are obvious. We can list all the reasons why we do and do not want to become more assertive. Since our motivation is totally conscious we can rationally describe the personal advantages and disadvantages of acting more boldly. But when it comes to following the exercises that will help us reduce our fear of exams, we are unable to pinpoint the reasons that we are not following through. All we know is that though we say we really hope to be rid of our exam phobia something seems to prevent us. Very likely, as shown in Chapter Three, unconscious opposing motives are blocking the way. In either case, whether conscious or unconscious drives are responsible for conflict, we will not bring about personality change until opposing motives are resolved.

There are many types and varieties of conflict. Sometimes we are in a quandary because two equally attractive goals are presented and to choose one requires losing the other. At other times, we are forced to make a choice between two unattractive, negative goals. For example, either we stick with the unpleasant job we have, or quit and put up with the harassment and lowered standard of living that comes with collecting unemployment checks. Psychologists have classified the different types of conflict, and though these descriptions are just a beginning, they help substantially in understanding our own opposing motives. As a first step, then, in learning to resolve our own conflicts, we should decide what kind of conflict we ourselves are experiencing. There are four fundamental types of conflict and these are described in the following pages.

Approach-Approach Conflict

Approach-approach conflict is a conflict between two or more equally attractive goals. Selecting either chocolate or strawberry ice-cream is such a conflict because both objectives are highly desirable. In a classic psychologic study at Yale University, two scientists, Carl Hovland and Robert Sears, demonstrated the motor effect of this kind of conflict. They provided subjects with a pencil and a square of paper, seated them at desks and instructed them to keep their pencils poised at a starting point on the paper. The paper was arranged on the desk so that each of the four corners had a green light. When the light in one of the corners flashed, they were to draw a pencil line to it. After the preliminary instructions, subjects were taught to respond quickly to flashing green lights in one or another corner. Once the participants had become accustomed to responding rapidly to a green light in this or that corner, the experimenter simultaneously flashed green lights in two different corners.

When two corners were lit up, subjects were unexpectedly confronted between having to choose between two approach goals. As it turned out, this was not really a difficult decision for most, since two thirds of the experimental participants quickly resolved this conflict. They simply picked one of the lights and moved towards it, ignoring the other. This is very much like our behavior when we choose strawberry as against chocolate. Both were positive goals and the conflict was not very serious.

In most cases, approach-approach conflict is easily solved. We recognize the distinct advantages of each target but since both goals are beneficial, it's not too hard to choose one at the expense of the other. Notice, though, that this is not true for all individuals. Even in the simple motor-conflict experiment, not all subjects moved towards one of the green lights and forgot the other. Actually, about a fifth of the subjects alternated. They drew a line towards one green light, then backed off and moved towards the other, and then back again, and again and again repeated this cycle. A tenth of the subjects tried for a compromise. They drew a line toward neither green light but instead between them. Still another tenth were helpless before the conflict; they could not resolve their dilemma in any way but sat staring blankly at the page or at the green lights. They asked for help but got none and were frozen into inaction.

The choice between two positives is not always simple or painless. Like the experimental subjects, we may alternate between two or more attractions so long that we are completely lost. A good student anxious to attend a leading university had very attractive offers from both Cornell and Princeton. He reported that both looked so' good that he kept changing his mind about which to accept. Ultimately, he hesitated so long that his deadline for acceptance passed and he was unable to choose either.

An approach-approach conflict may also surface when we are planning to make changes in our personality. Sometimes the trait we want clashes with another characteristic that, when we think about it, is equally desirable for us.

> Margaret had always wanted to be able to do well at a sport. She particularly liked tennis for it was an active game that, in addition to being fun, had many social advantages. Many of the more likeable and interesting people in her area played the game and could be found on the courts. Consequently, Margaret rearranged her schedule, planned practice sessions, chose good partners, programmed reinforcement and other learning contingencies. In short, she followed a good behavioral plan for personality change.
>
> Margaret got started on her program and for a while all went well. Then gradually she noticed that she was beginning to miss some of her tennis sessions. Several times she almost forgot about them. This was most likely to happen when she found herself reading. She knew she enjoyed reading but she liked tennis also and was surprised that she sometimes gave one up for the other.

In Margaret's case there was little hidden or unconscious about her motivation. All she needed to do was give her situation some thought and she easily recognized two approach goals. She heartily enjoyed reading and consumed at least one novel a week. At the same time, she sincerely wanted tennis and all the ádded benefits it would bring. But she could not do both, for Margaret's work and other activities limited her free time. Thus, she found herself in an approach-approach conflict. First, she followed through on the tennis, but then, missing her reading, she dropped tennis and went back to her books. And then bouncing back the other way, she dropped reading again to pursue tennis with vigor. Most people easily solve approach-approach conflicts, but those few that do not are caught, like Margaret, in an unhappy trap. They make little if any progress toward their goal and do not bring about any substantial personal change because they are unable to choose between two equally appealing behaviors.

Avoidance-Avoidance Conflict

To demonstrate avoidance-avoidance conflict, Sears and Hovland trained their subjects to draw a pencil line *away* from a red light flashed in a corner of their paper. Once the subjects were accustomed to drawing quickly away from the corner that flashed red, lights signaled red simultaneously at two different corners. Now subjects had an avoidance-avoidance conflict. They needed to escape from two opposing negative goals at the same time.

Faced with an avoidance-avoidance situation, nearly half of the experimental participants acted ineffectively. Instead of clearly avoiding one or the other, they hesitated or made small back and forth movements going nowhere. Instead of reacting decisively to one or another avoidant goal, subjects became motionless.

> Stan was soon to graduate from college. He looked forward to finishing since he had always been an indifferent student who had trouble studying, taking tests, and disciplining himself. However, as Stan got closer to graduation, he realized that he was faced with several choices he did not like. One, he could accept a job as a junior high school teacher. Two, he could stay at his college and enter a special two-year program for his master's degree. Since he liked neither of these alternatives, perhaps he could avoid both by just returning home and living with his parents. But since Stan was twenty-four-years-old and had been independent for some time, this did not seem an attractive alternative either.

Stan decided that the least negative goal was to return to school. He hoped that perhaps he could learn to improve his academic habits and become a better student. Consequently, he started a self-improvement program sponsored by his college. This was intended to help him teach himself to become a more motivated and effective graduate student.

After three weeks of graduate school, Stan dropped both his self-improvement and his schooling. He packed his belongings and moved home to live with his parents. He stayed at home for two months and then took a job as a substitute social studies teacher in a school system in a nearby city. Stan lasted on this job for little more than a month when he quit and tried to re-enroll in his graduate program in midyear. He was unsuccessful and ended up living with a former roommate and in his own words, "Doing nothing."

Stan is caught in the grip of an avoidance conflict. The three alternatives he believes are available are all equally repellent to him. He is very likely to repeat the cycle of leaving school, taking a job, depending on his parents, again and again, unless he finds a way to resolve his conflict.

Approach-Avoidance Conflict

To demonstrate the approach-avoidance conflict in the drawing experiment, a new group of participants was instructed to draw toward a green light and away from a red one. When the subjects were well trained, the experimenters switched tactics and flashed both a green and red light in the same corner. Subjects were now caught in an age-old classic conflict situation. They were both attracted and repelled by the same objective. In this type of experiment, subjects can be seen literally moving toward a goal, then backing away and moving toward it again. Some have called this the *yo-yo effect* since subjects alternately go forward and back, never quite reaching the goal but never backing off too far. The vacillation back and forth is explained by the attractants and repellents within the same target. The subject moves towards the goal because of its positive appeal. But the closer he moves, the more prominent the negative becomes, forcing him to move back. After backing off, the avoidant features dim and the attractive ones again loom large so that the forward movement is likely to be repeated, and so on.

Approach-avoidance conflicts are among the most common

of all dilemmas faced by people in real-life situations. We are attracted very strongly by a particular goal but once we really examine it, several negative features stand out that keep us away. The young man (Ed, in Chapter Three) who wanted to have his teeth repaired was caught in an approach-avoidance conflict. Consciously, he wanted to lose his dental phobia for good and substantial reasons. But unconsciously he wanted to hold on to his fear of dental work for other reasons that were important to his psychological make-up. The same kind of approach-avoidance conflict was true for Florence, whose ultimate goal was supposedly to save her marriage. But she learned that, without her knowing it, she was also driven to let her marriage disintegrate so that she could be free again. An excellent example of approach-avoidance behavior was demonstrated by Vivian, who also had a marriage conflict.

> Vivian was thirty-four, divorced, and had two small children. After living alone for three years she had decided to marry again since she believed she had found a man almost perfect for her. "He's easy-going, responsible, fun to be with, and acts like a father. I couldn't have found a better person for me." But as the wedding date neared, Vivian found a reason to postpone the formalities. "It's not a good time since the kids are still in school." When the summer vacation came Vivian once again asked to postpone the marriage, pleading she needed more time to prepare her daughter for the new relationship. During the next year Vivian found several more reasons to postpone the wedding so that altogether it was put off four times. Each time, however, Vivian strongly and apparently sincerely argued that she did want to get married and that her boyfriend was just the right person for her.

Vivian is oscillating back and forth in the typical approach-avoidance way. As she gets close to the goal, the negatives push her back. When she backs off, the positives pull her forward. Vivian is making decisions but they are conflicting ones that get her nowhere.

Double Approach-Avoidance Conflict

Before we discuss ways of resolving the various kinds of conflicts, one more type needs to be outlined. The double approach-avoidance conflict is a dilemma in which several goals contain both negative and positive elements. In the drawing experiment, double approach-avoidance was simulated by lighting both red and green signals at two corners of the drawing paper. Now subjects had a choice of two attractive goals, but each goal also had its repellants. In this situation, the great majority of experimental participants reacted ineffectively. They vacillated, hesitated, gave up, or remained almost totally unresponsive. They simply could not handle the pushes and pulls coming at them from several directions.

When human beings are faced with several goals each of which has positive as well as negative elements, the kind of conflict generated can result in the total breakdown of behavior. This happened to a young woman who was highly anxious about her sexuality. Although she considered herself heterosexual, she had several intimate experiences with women. Nevertheless, she remained attracted to men. If one accurately analyzed her situation, it was clear that both men and women were physically attractive to her but there were also negatives for both sexes. She was afraid of men and with women she felt guilt. Consequently, she continued to wander back and forth between the two with increasing apprehension and dissatisfaction. By the time she sought help she was so distraught that she was unable to relate to either sex.

The Signs of Conflict

If all our motives were always conscious, it would be easy to know whether or not we have a conflict. Say, for example, we decided it would be nice to be much more independent. However, we also like being fussed over, taken care of, and even controlled. Without much hesitation, we could easily label these opposing needs an approach-avoidance conflict. But we are not quickly or easily aware of opposing motives for they can be deeply hidden. As a result, we cannot depend upon instantly knowing whether our stated goals for change will conflict with some unspoken need that is unconscious. But once we start on our personality modification program, we can learn if we have ambivalent feelings. The behavioral signs of motivational conflict are unmistakable. If we have conflict, our own conduct and feelings will reveal it to us. Our behavior and emotions will signal that unconsciously or otherwise our personality objectives are running into opposition.

The most obvious evidence of conflict is procrastination, and its close twin, indecision. Like Vivian who kept putting back her wedding date, when we delay, rethink and put off, the odds are good that the goals that attract us also have some repellent elements that we may not recognize. Vivian herself did not know why she kept putting off her wedding date although she knew that from time to time her resolve to marry weakened.

> I don't really know if there is just one reason I put the date back. Each time I had a different reason that I think was a good one. I did feel a little undecided, now and again. That's why I put it off the second and third time especially. I wasn't sure I was doing the right thing. That last time I put it off too, was more than procrastination. Then I knew I wasn't sure. That's why I want to change my personality. So I can be sure and stop putting things off.

Indecisiveness is another clear sign of goal conflict. Recall the student who was accepted to both Cornell and Princeton. He kept weighing the advantages of one, and then the other. Maybe he ought to choose Cornell since it is such a good school and so nicely located. But then Princeton has so many advantages also. His indecisiveness ultimately cost him both opportunities. He wavered, thought and rethought so long that the deadline for acceptance passed before he made up his mind.

Vacillation, meaning in this case to sway to and fro, is another signal of conflict. First we go toward this goal and then we bounce back and go towards another. At one time we take up our new behaviors with enthusiasm and next time quickly drop them again. Margaret, who wanted to learn tennis, showed this kind of vacillation. She started her tennis program with energy but then petered out and found herself reading. Then she dropped reading and switched back to tennis. Stan also showed a great deal of bouncing back and forth. He began graduate school, dropped that and took a job. Next he went to live with his parents. Then he left them and reapplied to graduate school.

More disabling than either procrastination or vacillation is what may be called *freezing*. In the approach-avoidance experiments some subjects tried at first to move the pencil forward, then backed off and then tried again but eventually they were im-mobilized. Their hand gripped the pencil and sat rigidly still on the paper. The same thing eventually happened to Vivian. She set a marriage date and when asked if she intended to go through with it, said, "I don't know." Then when she was asked if she might not prefer to postpone the date again she also replied, "I don't know." She described herself as "coming to the end of the line. I just don't know what to do anymore." Vivian was immobilized. She could no longer act. She made no arrange-ments for the coming wedding, yet she did not oppose it or post-pone it. Like the experimental subjects who could not decide whether to approach or avoid the red-green goal, Vivian was frozen into inaction. Stan became similarly frozen. After being rejected from re-entering graduate school, he went to live with a former roommate. Here he did nothing, made no plans, and did not even think about his future. He existed solely on his room-mate's generosity.

The more serious the conflict, the more likely it is to result in symptoms of psychological distress. The person with powerful opposing drives may feel downcast, worried, restless, have trouble sleeping, be fatigued, extrasensitive, and suffer many other physical and emotional complaints. Of course, these symp-toms are also found in depression, anxiety, and other disorders, so that exact diagnosis should be left to professionals. But it is important to recognize that in a mild to moderate way, these dis-tress symptoms often accompany the procrastination and indeci-sion that are so typical of conflicting motivation. The young woman with the sexual dilemma suffered such distress symp-toms to a considerable degree.

> I find myself unable to relate to anyone now. I go around feeling depressed, sorry for myself. I have developed in-somnia. I lost weight and I'm tired all the time. I'm irri-table. I snap at people. I worry what's to become of me.

All these behaviors and emotions, from vacillation to worry to fatigue can indicate motivational conflict. When we embark on our personality change program and seem to put it off, start and stop again and again, or experience symptoms of distress, the chances are good that we are in a dilemma. Part of us wants to go ahead, to be more aggressive or less inhibited or fearful, but part of us does not. Our goal may seem logical and reasonable and one we have hoped and dreamt about for years. Yet when it comes to mustering the motivation to start and persist, things do not seem to work out. When this happens we now recognize our difficulties as signs of opposing drives. We know, then, that it is time to pause, examine our needs and solve our conflicts.

Solving Conflict

In the following pages, several general methods to resolve conflict are suggested. These techniques will be suitable for many situations and individuals. In addition, readers may find them useful to help stimulate creative solutions to their own particular and special conflicts.

Act Now   There is a folk saying, He who hesitates is lost. Like many such maxims, this contains a good bit of psychological wisdom. A behavior scientist of today might rephrase this, however: In an approach-approach conflict, act quickly. Recall the student who had a choice between Cornell and Princeton and thought it over so long that he lost both opportunities. Had he acted with deliberate speed he would not have been in the unhappy situation of losing everything.

Acting quickly and decisively is valid mainly in situations where the choices are equally, or nearly equally positive. If all the alternatives are close to being identical you can't lose choosing any one of them. But if you hesitate too long you may well end up losing all. Hence, first define whether or not the alternatives are equally desirable. If they are, then go ahead. Move rapidly and with determination and the chances are excellent that you will be pleased with the outcome.

Strengthen or Weaken a Motive   One reason that many people have conflict is because they have not thoroughly examined the power of their conflicting motives. Consequently, they seem to want to do A and B with just about the same amount of enthusiasm. But if they thoroughly investigated both A and B, they might find that one of them actually has slightly different attractive (or repellent) strength. In the previous chapter it was pointed out that unconscious motives frequently conflict with conscious ones. The means for ferreting out unconscious feelings were presented. These same techniques, useful for making us aware of hidden needs, can also be employed to help us strengthen (or weaken) particular motives.

> A successful engineer had an offer of promotion to a supervisory post, provided he was willing to move to another plant, five hundred miles away. He liked the idea but as he began to plan his move he found himself very much attached to his present location and his family home. The engineer said, "It wasn't simply a matter of choosing between two attractive possibilities. I definitely wanted to go and also definitely to stay. At the same time, I had some feeling that if only I could figure it out better, one or the other would win out."

The engineer entered counseling and during his third session several anxieties about relocating came out. Most important was his fear about leaving his own home. He had a childhood scarred by very serious, sometimes even violent parental quarrels. When he was only seven his father stormed out of the house and was never heard from again. For his mother and consequently for him, the house became the symbol and substance of all the security they had. In fact, the engineer still lived in this same house with his own family.

As the engineer's old feelings about his parental home became clear, he lost much of his anxiety about moving. The strength of his motive to remain thereby decreased and the potency of his desire to become a supervisor increased commensurately. Ultimately, with further exploration of his motives, he was able to sell his old house and move.

Motive can also be strengthened or weakened by methods that are fully conscious and rational. What this requires is simply that we seek as much information as possible about the various alternatives that seem to conflict. Remember Margaret, who wanted both to play tennis and to read. She was advised to reexamine both motives very carefully and write down the advantages of each.

> I made a long list of all the things I liked about tennis and all the things I liked about reading. I arranged them in priorities and assigned them points and it all balanced out.

Margaret followed a technique that is frequently used. She jotted down her reasons for wanting each goal and assigned a point value (from 1 to 10) for each reason. For example, she decided that reading as "fun" and tennis as "fun" were both worth 8 points each. The social value of tennis was graded 4 points while reading earned only 1 point.

> Everything seemed to balance out pretty closely. I had 26 points for tennis and 24 for reading. Too close to make a decision. Then I read an article on fitness, because I was searching for more information about tennis. It said that tennis has enormous aerobic and body benefits. It burns off so many calories, does wonders for the shape of your legs, and even helps your complexion. I always do want to look better so I gave that 9 points. So tennis had 35 points and was way ahead of reading.

Margaret developed as much information about tennis and reading as she could. Finally she found an incentive, a healthier trimmer body and figure, that enormously strengthened her motive to play tennis. Thus, she was able to make a decision and stick with it. It is not necessary to devise a point system but it is necessary to list all the reasons for wanting one or another goal. Then, when the two seem equally balanced, seek further. Find out as much as possible about each alternative and the chances are good you will develop information that will significantly strengthen (or weaken) a particular desire, making the final choice fairly easy.

Leave the Field   When experimental psychologists force a white rat into a box with a choice of only two negative goals, the animal tries as hard as it can to get out of the box entirely. Sometimes, even when an approach-approach conflict is created, experimental participants, both human and animal, just give up and leave the field. They can not solve the problem and decide it best to just leave the entire situation behind. This behavior can be consciously copied for it is often a worthwhile approach to solving a motivational dilemma. Just get out of the situation and use your new freedom to examine other alternatives.

> Vivian had a classic approach-avoidance conflict. She both wanted and did not want to marry. The result was that she

would set a date to marry and as that approached she would postpone it. She did this four times in all, till she herself, and her future husband were disappointed and confused. Vivian finally decided that she could not endlessly repeat this cycle. She informed her suitor that she did not want to marry and would also stop seeing him. Although she liked him a great deal, she pointed out that she needed to approach her situation from a different angle. She was going to stop all her relationships for quite some time, go into an encounter group and try to understand herself as a person and a woman.

When we leave the field, we open ourselves to entirely new choices. We get out of a situation that has proved frustrating and begin all over again. Sometimes the new experiences and insights we have will enable us to go back and solve the dilemma that caused us to leave, but often as not both our situations and personal characteristics change and we are no longer drawn into unsolvable conflicts. Vivian described this situation when she said:

> After I called a halt to my bouncing back and forth about marrying, my life really took off. In six months I found a new me. I was no longer that dizzy inadequate-feeling typical middle-class girl that had to be married to be fulfilled. Now I feel a new me. I have a positive outlook on myself as a woman and as a sexual person. I like me and I have moved way beyond worrying about marrying or not marrying.

Analyze Avoidants   Stan did not like living with his parents, returning to school, or keeping a job. The result was that he ended up living with a friend and doing "nothing." Eventually, he entered counseling and was helped to look at each goal he disliked and analyze why he disliked it. When he carefully considered continued schooling and living with his parents, their avoidant nature seemed reasonable and appropriate. But when he talked about working, it appeared as if the major reason he avoided a job was that he had difficulty getting along with supervisors. He actually liked the independence and financial reward of working but was afraid and resentful of his immediate superiors. He had never learned to get along with a boss. This difficulty was a solvable problem. Stan was helped to define the behaviors he was talking about and learned techniques that would enable him to cooperate with his supervisor. In this way, the negative value of one of the goals, working, was greatly diminished, and Stan was enabled to make a choice.

Whenever we are faced with an avoidance-avoidance or double approach-avoidance conflict, we should try to dissect the avoidant elements. Exactly what feelings (conscious and unconscious) keep us away from this goal. Very often we will find some attitudes that can be significantly modified and thus decrease the repellent nature of a particular choice.

Listen to Your Body Very often we force ourselves into a conflict. We think we want both A and B but the only reason we think this is because we are trying to impress ourselves. We have previously described a young woman who was very distraught about her sexual experiences with both men and women. She finally became so confused about her sexuality that she was seriously depressed and avoided people altogether. In counseling some of her feelings of depression were relieved and she was encouraged to reestablish her relationships. But she was cautioned also to observe herself closely. To listen to her body and understand its responses. After several months of counseling, this client reported:

> It's clear to me now. I enjoy being with women very much. I'm relaxed and yet I'm turned on. My body likes being there. I like men too but it's not the same thing. I am tense. My body is saying "I don't want this." I know I am doing it only for appearances. I was trying to convince myself that I was as heterosexual as the next person but my body wasn't buying it.

We often feel similar body signals when we move toward our own conflicting goals. We may think we want both A and B but let's actually move closer and try A and then B. How do we feel? Does A or does B actually "feel" better? Perhaps we have several goals that have both approach and avoidance elements. Stop speculating! Instead of wondering whether one or the other might be better give them a little try and study yourself very carefully. Which felt good and which left you uneasy. When we are on the beach it is of little use wondering whether or not to go in the water because it looks cold. The only way to solve that dilemma is to stick in an inquisitive toe and let the chill (or warmth) decide our next action.

Life Goals Too often we treat an approach or avoidance conflict as if it existed all by itself. We forget that a lifetime lies ahead of us. Perhaps then we ought to carefully consider the various possibilities open to us in the context of an entire lifetime. Forget about how we feel now towards this or that approach or avoidant objective. Consider instead how that particular goal fits in with overall self-concept, our long-term ideas and ambitions.

> Ray had been married for only eighteen months when he met Carol. At first they saw each other only at work but gradually they secretly began spending time together afterwards. Before too long, Ray said he was "deeply in love" with Carol. But he did not want to leave his own wife either for he stated very strongly that he loved her too. Ray was pushed into a dilemma since both women were aware of the situation and were unwilling to share his affections. Both the wife and the girl friend agreed that Ray had to choose between them. Ray could think of a good many pluses and minuses for each of the women. His wife was very warm, interested in their home, gentle, and supportive. On the negative side, she was not very athletic, uninterested in parties or socializing, and was three years older than Ray. Ray's girl friend's distinctive positive features were that she was very creative, loved the outdoors, and had a good job and income. Her particular minuses were that she disliked any kind of homemaking job or role, was too independent, and could be very impulsive. In addition, both women had strong attractants in the way they were sensual, intelligent, and uninhibited. The result was that Ray found himself in a double approach-avoidance conflict. There were two choices and both had their positive and negative features.

The conflict Ray was faced with was not soluble through any of the usual resolution procedures. Ray examined his motives, both conscious and unconscious. He arranged his needs in terms of their point value and obtained as much information about both women as he could. Still no resolution was forthcoming. Ray's therapist asked him to think about his long-range goals. What were his life plans? After describing his future work, home, and hobbies, Ray finally seemed to fasten on something of significance.

I know I want a nice-size family. Not now but when I'm a few years older. I want to have children. I want four all together. And if we can't have them we'll adopt them. I know that's how I see the rest of my life. I love children, their games and talk and things. . . . From the time the first one is born for the next twenty or twenty-five years I'll be a father, till the kids are old enough to start their own families. And then I want to be a grandfather. I want that. I always have. That's my long-range plan. . .

Once Ray was enabled to see his entire life, his choice between wife and girl friend became easier. His girl friend was essentially uninterested in children and family. His wife, on the other hand, was strongly motivated to raise a family. Being forced to choose one or the other, Ray could now decide on the basis of his long-term goals.

Conclusion

Frequently when we make plans to change our behavior we discover that we are making little progress because of a motivational conflict. We both want and do not want a particular objective or else a contrary motive is subtly interfering with our desire to change. In Chapter Three we learned how to uncover motives that may unconsciously sabotage our "willpower," meaning our conscious wishes and desires. In this chapter a number of ways have been suggested that help resolve conflict. When we have uncovered our uncertainties and become aware of our mixed feelings, then we are ready to work out solutions and move ahead to change our personalities and our lives.

Five
How-
Change
through
Reinforcement

In this chapter the first technique for changing personality will be explained. This method makes use of the age-old observation that when you reward someone's conduct he is likely to act the same way again. The reward can be as obvious as paying a youngster to wash your car, thus assuring he will come around asking to do it again. Or the reward may be subtle. Notice, for example, how when we smile encouragingly to the person talking to us, they tell more and more. Psychologists have rediscovered the potency of reward and through extensive research verified just how powerfully effective it is in ruling our behavior.

Reinforcement

Behavior that is rewarded persists. In fact almost any behavior, even the most arbitrarily selected conduct, continues and increases if it is rewarded. To give you just some idea of the range of human actions that can be made to increase by reward here are just two examples:

> Young adult men and women were under the impression that they were being interviewed by a psychologist about their career plans. In actuality the psychological interviewers each picked out one of the subject's mannerisms and subtly rewarded it. Mannerisms selected included stroking the chin; pulling hair; scratching head, saying, "you know"; and looking the interviewer directly in the eye. These behaviors were rewarded by the interviewer's smiling slightly, nodding and saying, "Hm, hm." The result of this

project was that the targeted behaviors for all subjects increased throughout the interview. In addition, none of the subjects was aware that they were being rewarded or that any of their behaviors had increased.

Frieda hated to do housework but she loved to visit neighbors, drink coffee, and gossip. Through a friend who was knowledgeable about the effects of reward, she worked out the following scheme. For each hour she effectively cleaned her house, ironed, washed, and cooked, she was entitled to fifteen minutes of visiting. Frieda kept honest records and soon found herself working four hours a day and visiting one hour.

Rewarded behavior persists and almost anything can serve as a reward. A nod of the head, a smile, a fifty-dollar bonus, a visit with a neighbor or an ice-cream may all strengthen particular behaviors. Let's be scientific and use the word *reinforcer*, instead of *reward*, since it is a broader, more general term. We can now understand two important psychological rules. First, *reinforcement causes behavior to persist*. This means that willingly or not, consciously or otherwise, behavior that is reinforced will likely continue and increase. The second rule is that *almost any event may be a reinforcer*. Nearly all responses, reactions, stimuli or whatever, *directly following a particular behavior* have the potential for acting as reinforcers.

Through reinforcement we can make profound and enduring changes in our behavior and personality. But we have to know a little more about reinforcement to do so. Remember that reinforced behavior persists, and most things can be reinforcers. Knowing only this, Jack and Jill, two unsuccessful agriculture students, decided to reinforce their studying behavior. Their program was to allow themselves to listen to their stereo for one hour for every two hours they studied. The plan worked beautifully for Jill. But in his room, Jack studied little more than necessary, and then lost interest. He really did not look forward to listening to his stereo but preferred instead to wander into town and drink at a local tavern.

The case of Jack illustrates a third rule concerning reinforcement. Yes, any stimulus could be a reinforcer. But for every person there must be an individual assessment of its value. A reinforcer that works for Abe might not work for Babe. *A reinforcer is any event that has potency for you*. Jack chose an event, listening to his stereo, that had almost no potency for him. After the first one or two unsuccessful attempts to study he should have carefully reexamined his reinforcer.

Fortunately for Jack, Jill knew that if a reinforcer is to successfully influence behavior, it must prove its strength for that particular person. Since studying was difficult for Jack, what sort of behavior might offer sufficient inducement for him to study? Jill talked to Jack in terms of what he particularly enjoyed. He was meticulously groomed—always neatly shaven, very well dressed, deodorized, kempt, and coiffured. He agreed that henceforth, after getting up in the morning, he would wear yesterday's clothes, not shave or otherwise clean until he had completed his quota of study for that day. Being extremely neat was very important to Jack so that this reinforcer worked very well. Jack studied more and more and eventually he and Jill graduated.

The reinforcer chosen in your own behavior-change program must be meaningful and strong enough to really motivate you. It is no use choosing an ice-cream cone as a reward when you are quite indifferent to this inducement. Select a reinforcer that is a valued, significant and vital event for you. But the reinforcer must be manageable. It is no use promising yourself a yacht. Certainly a seventy-five-foot boat may be a highly desirable object but it is not within easy grasp. It is not an event that can be readily controlled.

A fourth rule for changing behavior through reinforcement is that the reinforcer must be *manageable*. The consequence following the behavior chosen for strengthening must be certain and predictable. This was not done by a salesman who promised himself a new car if he met his sales quota. While he was working hard, knocking on more doors and selling more aggressively than ever before, it occurred to him that no matter how much he sold he could not afford to buy a new car anyway. He was so disappointed that he stopped selling altogether. This salesman had chosen a reinforcer, like a new yacht, that was not obtainable.

> Tess lived with her mother and tended to quibble and scrap with her a great deal. Her mother was aging and Tess felt bad that she fought so much. She decided that whenever she could complete a set number of hours with her mother without fighting she would reinforce herself by going out

and playing tennis. First Tess planned to be free of quibbling till 11 A.M., then noon, 1 P.M., before allowing herself tennis. For the first two days Tess did not fight and left the house at 11 A.M. to play tennis. On the first day she met an old friend and they enjoyed a vigorous two hours of playing. On the second day, few players were around and Tess had to settle for playing with an older man who was very poor. On several subsequent tennis days she sometimes had a good time but all too often she was lonely, undermatched, or frustrated by her game. Eventually she abandoned her behavior-change project and decided that she just could not learn to get along better with her mother.

There was little wrong with Tess's plan for change, but she did select the wrong reinforcer. Tennis had sufficient potency for Tess but it was not manageable. There was no way of assuring that when her behavior was appropriate, the game that followed would be satisfactory. She might not have a good partner, it could rain or the courts all be taken. Tess could not control her reinforcer, hence it was a poor choice.

Any consequence can be a reinforcer but it must be both important to, and controllable by you. Here are some reinforcers that others have used and found individually effective. They are not arranged in any special order but simply a selection to indicate the wide variety of consequences that could serve as reinforcers. This is by no means a complete list. It is a sample that should help readers think of consequences that might be individually suitable for them. After reading this selection, make a list of reinforcers that are suitable for you.

Sports: jogging, playing basketball, hunting, fishing, swimming.
Cleanliness: showering, perfuming, ironing, dusting, moving furniture.
Shopping: exotic foods, clothing, records, auto parts.
Eating: pastry, cookies, nuts, fruit, steak, candy.
Drinking: fine wine, liquor, soft drinks, lemonade, milk, beer.
Performing: playing instrument, acting, singing.
Recreation: reading, playing cards, crossword puzzles, listening to music, watching TV.
Outdoors: hiking, gardening, horse-back riding, bird-watching.
Sex: flirting, nude pictures, movies, masturbating, adult literature, dancing.

Miscellaneous: taking a course, photography, travel, letter writing, gossiping, smiling, praying, meditating, sleeping, collecting, painting, boasting, competing, visiting, finishing a project.

Reinforcement and Pleasure

It is easy to suppose that anything, and everything, that gives pleasure is a reinforcer. This is in large part a correct assumption. But, as we have learned, for a reinforcer to do its work, it must be both potent and controllable. Thus not absolutely everything that gives pleasure is actually a reinforcer. Not all consequences no matter how pleasurable they may seem are guaranteed to help us change our behavior. Each and every reinforcer must be carefully and individually measured in terms of what it can do for us.

Our tendency to think of pleasure and reinforcement as identical, needs to be revised in one additional way. *All reinforcers are not directly pleasurable.* There are very many ways to modify our behavior without having the reinforcer necessarily feeling good, being pleasing, or fun.

> Gary had a low back problem. His physician prescribed thirty minutes of exercise nightly before going to bed. Gary wanted to strengthen his back but seldom seemed to be able to work in his exercises before retiring. Since Gary showered every night his showering was made dependent on his exercising. He could not shower unless he first exercised. This plan worked well and Gary soon exercised regularly every night.

This case illustrates a discovery made about reinforcers by a psychologist named David Premack, long with Ohio State University. Premack noticed that any *behavior that is frequently performed can be used to reinforce any less frequent behavior.* Gary *always* took a shower. He had accustomed himself to this routine before he could go to sleep. This made it simple to link new behavior to the shower-taking. Gary now could not take a shower until he completed his exercise. The shower, a relatively neutral, innocuous but habitual routine, became a powerful reinforcer. Or, as Premack would have pointed out, the frequently performed behavior (showering) had been used to reinforce a new behavior (exercising).

Premack's observation is potentially very useful for those planning to change their personalities. It relieves them of the sometimes difficult problem of searching for a reinforcer that is strong, manageable and pleasurable. Now they need merely to look at what they do everyday, what behaviors are a constant part of their existence, and use one of these as a reinforcer. Here is another instance where frequent behavior was used as a reinforcer.

> A foreign service trainee was learning another language. He was to review what he had learned each day while lying in bed, before going to sleep. He reported however that whenever he lay down he would start having erotic fantasies and forget about his language lessons. He wanted to get rid of his fantasies in order to help review his materials. But he was advised instead to keep his fantasy and use it as a reinforcer. His new plan consisted of sitting up in bed reviewing all his language instruction for that day. When that was finished he allowed himself to lie down and fantasize.

Another way of reinforcing your own target behavior is through a token system. Use chips or pieces of paper and assign a value to each. Then devise a scale that will give you one token for each desired behavior. When you have ten tokens, for instance, you can buy yourself a new shirt; for forty tokens you get a whole suit. The tokens have no immediate pleasurable consequence but they are cumulative. Here is how a couple used a token system to change their lives.

> Jack and Stella complained that though they loved each other they were sexually incompatible. When the counselor asked them to specify their difficulty in terms of behavior in a situation, two complaints emerged. Jack said that Stella did not agree to intercourse often enough. Stella complained that Jack spent too little time on foreplay and also reached orgasm too quickly. A token system was devised using poker chips. Stella was to give Jack 0, 1, or 2 poker chips depending upon, first, how long he continued foreplay and second, how long he delayed his climax. If, for example, both foreplay and orgasm delay were as much as Stella desired she was to give Jack six chips. In turn Jack could have intercourse with Stella, cash in his chips, at any time, whenever he had accumulated five. After a slow beginning, the length of foreplay and intercourse soon increased and as

a result, of course, so did the frequency of coitus, to the satisfaction of both partners.

Money is a universal token system. Jack and Stella could have used money but in their situation, employing dollars might have amusing but also unfortunate connotations. Nevertheless in less delicate circumstances people have reinforced their behavior by giving themselves coins or bills according to a schedule they have prepared in advance. One woman who was intent on dieting, for example, carefully calculated how much less food she ate in terms of dollars and cents and gave herself this money to spend "foolishly and wildly," at the end of each month. One month she had enough to buy an extravagant, hand-sewn leather hat, an indulgence she would not have permitted herself before.

But what happens when you are completely lost for a reinforcer? You have looked down the list and nothing has seemed appropriate. You may even have tried some sort of token or money system and that too did not work. There is one last alternative and it partly uses the principle previously discussed, of using a frequent behavior.

> Barry was forty-six years old, married and had worked in a subordinate position in an accounting firm for seventeen years. He had never risen because he had never managed to pass his examinations for Certified Public Accountant. Now he had determined to be more ambitious, and the first behavioral hurdle was studying for his examination. He went to the library every night to read appropriate books but always found himself distracted. Usually he drifted over to the recreational section and spent his time reading science fiction or looking at magazines.

Barry believed that nothing could force him to study. But then he was instructed to keep track of his study time and his recreational reading. Next he was taught to divide his time so that for every twenty minutes studying he could read recreationally for ten. At first he studied only ten minutes and recreation for five. Within two weeks however he was studying for ninety minutes at a time. Barry was using the behavior that *interfered* with his target behavior as a reinforcer. Thus when you seem to be entirely at a loss for something to use as a reinforcer, ask yourself, "What behaviors do I perform *instead* of my target?" You may find that there are all sorts of things you do, instead of what you should be doing. And all these diversions, whether they be watching girls, fingernail biting, sleeping, talking, or whatever, have the potential for being turned into reinforcers.

Analyze Reinforcement

When any behavior is reinforced it persists. This rule applies not only to the behavior we want to learn, but also to behavior we want to be rid of. In other words it may occasionally happen that behavior we do not want, continues to plague us because we are *unknowingly* reinforcing it. Here's a simple example of reinforcing undesirable behavior.

> Mrs. Meyer complained that her four-year-old son had "atrocious" eating habits. After considerable questioning, Mrs. Meyer specified her son's tendency to eat with his fingers and not use his fork. Mrs. Meyer was asked to describe in complete detail several typical eating periods so that what was actually happening could be understood. It became clear that the mother was actually reinforcing finger eating. Whenever her child ate with a fork, she said nothing. But when he ate with his hands she would say, "Our little monkey," or laugh or otherwise in a very benign way indicate her disapproval.

Notice that this mother thought she was indicating disapproval of her child's habit of eating with his fingers. Actually she was reinforcing his finger use by calling attention to it. She should have been doing the opposite, and when instructed in this direction the mother learned quickly. She began to ignore her son's finger eating but instead when he did use his fork said, "Good boy," or gave similar reinforcements. In this way the child's use of the fork increased rapidly.

It is possible that behavior we want to change can be altered solely by eliminating reinforcers that have escaped our notice. Therefore in order to change our personality, instead of acquiring new behaviors, we may just have to stop reinforcing old ones. The following is the case of a divorced man named Steve who said he wanted to become more socially assertive. He claimed that he had always been shy and that after eight years of marriage had lost nearly all of his few social skills. Specifically at parties and other social gatherings Steve found himself alone and in a corner. He wanted, instead, to be able to talk and mingle with the other men and women. He had attempted various techniques to make himself more assertive and outgoing but nothing had worked. Steve was instructed in the nature of reinforcement and assigned the task of observing his own behavior very carefully. After *attending* to himself at several social gatherings, Steve observed the following.

> What I usually do is hang around the edges of the crowd. I try to talk a little but I guess I speak too softly. Usually nobody pays much attention to me. I notice that I try to get into the group for only a very little while. I give up very fast. I go to the kitchen, or wherever they have the food and I start eating. I sit by myself or I hang around a corner and I eat and that's how I spend a lot of the evening.

What Steve is doing is reinforcing his withdrawal through food. He makes a few feeble efforts to join in the fun and then isolates himself. Then he powerfully reinforces his isolation with food which is a very fundamental, exceedingly effective reinforcer. No wonder that he spends less and less time trying to socialize and more and more time alone and eating. The behavior he is reinforcing is isolation, and consequently, like other reinforced behavior, it is increasing.

What needed to be done with Steve was to reverse the reinforcement pattern. From now on Steve was not allowed to eat when alone. He was permitted food only in company. Steve was assigned the task of conducting a conversation, getting food, returning to the person talked to and then eating while socializing. At parties people continually eat while standing around and talking and Steve was instructed to follow this pattern.

> It worked like a hundred-dollar watch. I stopped myself from eating when alone. I started talking with someone and then after I had made that contact and we were really into something, then I allowed myself to nibble. The important thing was I did not reinforce my being alone anymore.

In quite a few instances all that is needed in order for us to change our personality and way of life is to analyze our reinforcement situation. Are we in effect reinforcing behavior that we do not want? Are some of our undesirable sexual, emotional, or habitual behaviors persistent only because we are unwittingly reinforcing them? Remember reinforcement does not have to be reward in the sense of having something very pleasurable happen to us. Behavior can be reinforced simply by paying attention to it, by noticing it, or following it with other behavior that is frequent or even remotely desirable. In the following case, for example, the reinforcement was in no sense a reward, yet it was as effective as the most pleasurable experience.

> Annie wanted very much to rid herself of her insistent nail-biting. She had tried putting pepper on her nails and otherwise punishing herself, but all to no avail. She was asked to describe her nail biting in detail and it turned out that she limited herself to four or five sessions a week. "I bite my nails at different times. Sometimes after lunch and again at night. If you want the behavior in detail, here's what I do. After lunch I sit at my desk. I also scratch my head a lot. Then I don't want to, but I'll start looking at my nails. Then I see this one is a little rough or longer and I'll bite it off to match the other one. Or I'll even bite some of the skin around the nails. Someone told me its helps my digestion. Do you think that has anything to do with it? Anyway I'll bite for a while, then I'll brush my teeth and settle down and do whatever work I have to do.

After hearing Annie's complete description it turned out that nail-biting was almost always followed by brushing teeth. Annie believed this the hygenic thing to do, but more important, she brushed her teeth as a matter of constant routine. In this instance, tooth brushing, a very frequent behavior, acted as a reinforcer to nail-biting. Annie was advised therefore that she was no longer to brush her teeth after nail-biting. She had to wait at least three hours after nail-biting to brush her teeth. As a result the nail-biting soon decreased. Remember therefore that before attempting very complex or radical behavior change, look first to see if just eliminating some hidden reinforcer may not result in bringing about the kind of personality change you want.

Extinction

In the foregoing analysis of reinforcement, a great deal of the time we have been talking about a process called extinction. When Annie stopped brushing her teeth after nail-biting her biting behavior soon ceased. When reinforcement is stopped, causing the formerly reinforced behavior to decrease, the process is called extinction. Annie was extinguishing her nail-biting behavior by no longer reinforcing it. In the same way, the mother who no longer paid attention to her son's eating with his fingers quickly extinguished the behavior. This leads us to the general rule that almost any behavior can be extinguished if the reinforcement is eliminated. So far we have seen how nail-biting, eating with fingers, and, to an extent, social isolation, were extinguished through non-reinforcement. Even fantasy behavior can be extinguished.

> Ben was a nineteen year old who was concerned about his disturbing sexual fantasies. As a younger adolescent he had gotten hold of several books and pictures that dealt with sadomasochism. Over the past few years he had seemed to grow more and more interested in this literature and sought out this type of material. He read the books, looked at the pictures, fantasized and became so aroused that he masturbated. Ben did not feel comfortable with this type of fantasy and wanted to have "normal" sexual ideas.

Masturbation is a profoundly pleasurable reinforcer. Ben was continually reinforcing his sadomasochistic reading and ideation. If he wanted to be rid of it he should no longer reinforce it by masturbation. But this was easier said than done. Ben had learned about reinforcement and extinction. He tried therefore to look at his sadomasochistic collection and not follow it by masturbation. But this seldom worked for just handling the books got Ben so aroused that he almost always masturbated.

For Ben a way needed to be found that would enable him to look at sadomasochistic erotica without stimulating him to masturbate. Ben himself devised an excellent extinction procedure. If he was sufficiently sexually deprived, "normal" pornography (*Playboy* and similar magazines) could also excite him to the point of satisfactory masturbation. Hence his plan was to read conventional erotica, masturbate, and repeat this performance as often as possible. Then when he was sexually exhausted he went back to his sadomasochistic collection. Since he was totally sexually spent each time he turned to the sadomasochistic readings, Ben slowly but steadily extinguished the impact of this material. After several months he reported very few sadomasochistic fantasies and the material itself had lost its arousal value.

Reinforcement Frequency

In order for reinforcement to work it does not have to be constant. Remember the mother who was unknowingly reinforcing her child's eating with his fingers. She tended to look at her child, make a facetious remark or sometimes scold him when he used his fingers. But she did not always do this. Sometimes she actually ignored him when he used his fingers to eat. The woman who bit her nails and followed it with toothbrushing was also mildly inconsistent. In nine out of ten cases she followed up a biting session with brushing, but 10 percent of the time she felt too busy or tired to brush.

These examples illustrate that in order for reinforcement to work it need not be total. Behavior that is reinforced most of the time is learned and retained, as well as, or even better than, behavior that is reinforced all the time. Notice that we have said that behavior that is partially reinforced may even be learned better than behavior totally reinforced. Psychological research shows that in most instances behavior reinforced about 80 percent of the time, is much more resistent to extinction than behavior constantly reinforced. This is usually illustrated by teaching two laboratory rats, alike in every respect, to jump through a hoop for a reinforcement consisting of a pellet of food. Rat A is given the pellet fifty times for fifty jumps. Rat B is given the pellet at uneven intervals forty times, for fifty jumps. Then after fifty jumps both animals are put on extinction trials. Neither animal A or B will get any more pellets of foods as a reinforcement for jumping. How long will the behavior persist now that extinction has begun? Animal A will likely jump another ten to fifteen times before his behavior ceases. Animal B, reinforced only part of the time, is likely to continue jumping twenty, thirty or more times before his behavior ceases. Partial reinforcement results in behavior that is more, much more difficult to extinguish.

The fact that partially reinforced behavior is much more persistent should teach us two things. First if we want to extinguish our behavior, never, never, reinforce it again, even briefly. If we do that then we have put ourselves on a partial reinforcement schedule and we will have tremendous difficulty getting rid of our behavior. Such was the unhappy case with

Annie. She stopped brushing her teeth following nail biting for a total of eight trials. She was well along the path to extinction. Then during her ninth nail-biting session she felt so unclean and unhygenic that she yielded to the temptation to brush her teeth. Following the tenth, eleventh, and twelfth nail-biting, Annie did not brush but she did again after her thirteenth, nineteenth and twenty-fifth biting session. Annie was in effect no longer extinguishing her nail-biting but partially reinforcing it, thus making it very likely her nail-biting would strengthen and persist.

It is absolutely critical, once extinction begins, not to make any exception. Mrs. Meyer, unlike Annie, was unswerving in her extinction plan. Once she learned that she was actually reinforcing her child's eating with his fingers she then totally ignored his use of his hands. She never again laughed at, noticed or in any way reinforced the undesired behavior. Thus her child's eating with his fingers stopped fairly quickly.

The critical rule concerning partial reinforcement is that when we want to extinguish behavior, never reinforce it again. A corollary rule is in order to learn new behavior reinforcement need not be totally continuous. Steve, who wanted to learn to socialize at parties, reinforced himself by eating whenever he talked with another. He did not need to do this all the time. He had to start with a chain of say five to ten continuous reinforcements and then he could occasionally skip a few reinforcements. In other words he, and we, can make use of the fact that partially reinforced behavior is as effectively learned, and often more so, then totally reinforced behavior.

Ending Reinforcement

Is Steve always going to have to eat in order to socialize? Is Gary always going to have to shower in order to do his exercises? Will Jack and Stella forever have to keep exchanging tokens in order to have a satisfactory sexual relationship? These questions that seem appropriate to a television soap opera are important to us. They ask whether or not reinforcement will have to continue forever in order to retain desirable behavior. The answer to all these questions is no! Eventually desirable behavior generates a momentum of its own. Steve found socializing more and more reinforcing in and of itself and eating became a smaller and smaller part of his party behavior. Gary, Jack and Stella all eventually found their target behaviors rewarding so that planned reinforcers were no longer needed. What seems to happen in most cases is that the desired behavior needed the impetus of the original reinforcers. Then after a while, other behavior associated with the desirable action itself become reinforcing. Steve put this very clearly when he said:

> I don't need food anymore to make me socialize. Now I catch myself in the middle of a group and we're talking to each other and I get this warm glow of satisfaction. Just being looked in the eye by someone else is a good experience.

Conclusion

Behavior that is rewarded persists. Therefore carefully specify the behavior that you want and reinforce it. Be certain too that you do the reverse. Clearly detail the behavior you do not want and make certain that you no longer reinforce that. Extinguish undesirable actions and reinforce desirable ones. Reinforcement can be a pleasurable reward or it can be simply behavior that is frequent. But to work, reinforcement must have meaning and be manageable and potent for you individually. Finally, a point we have not sufficiently stressed in this chapter but worthwhile restating is: keep records! Return to Chapter Two for a discussion of the techniques of record-keeping. Whenever you plan to add new behaviors, or drop old ones, the process of recording your progress is often by itself a highly effective reinforcement.

Six

How-
Punishing
Unwanted
Behavior

In the previous chapters we saw that reinforcement strengthens behavior. When any human act or action is rewarded, that behavior persists and even increases. And the reward need not be directly pleasurable. A reinforcement can be effective even if it is subtle or emotionally neutral. Since reward increases target behavior, it seems logical to suppose that punishment decreases selected actions. This is obviously a widely held assumption since every time a parent spanks a child, or a policeman issues a traffic ticket, they are assuming the effectiveness of punishment. Punishment does decrease behavior, but not always and worse yet, sometimes causes very unpleasant feelings or results. *Punishment is a powerful but tricky method of changing behavior so that we will have to treat it with great care.*

If we want to rid ourselves of some annoying habit such as nail-biting, or bed-wetting, or even stop ourselves from being inhibited or argumentative, then it may seem reasonable to punish those undesired responses. It might appear, on the surface, that all we need to do is specify the behavior we want to diminish and directly punish it. But as the following examples illustrate, punishment of our own behavior is not guaranteed to work.

> Kimble, an electronics technician, had two annoying habits that he believed impaired his social life and career progress. He bit his nails and he made a grimacing motion with his mouth and nose and sniffed like a child with a cold and no

handkerchief. Since Kim was familiar with some aspects of
how behavior is learned and unlearned, he built himself a
clever, pocket-sized, battery-run shock apparatus. He kept
the contraption in his pocket and whenever he bit his nails
or sniffled he administered himself a mild electric shock. At
first, shocking his undesired behavior seemed to work and
Kimble was proud of his invention. But slowly the tide
turned and Kim found himself forgetting to administer self-
shocks, letting the battery run down, and otherwise losing
interest in the project. At the end of five weeks the target behaviors were as strong as ever.

Garth had examined his behavior very carefully and decided
that his difficulties were due to his aggressiveness and
exhibitionism. Whether at work, at home or at a party he
demanded the center of the stage, talked endlessly and as a
consequence irritated a great many people. Garth decided
therefore that he should punish his exhibitionism and over-
talkativeness. His original resolve began at a party. When
he found himself too verbose he decided right then and
there to punish himself. The idea occurred to him that since
he disliked salted peanuts, whenever he talked too much or
demanded too much attention, he would have to eat three
handfuls of salted nuts. Garth's scheme worked fairly well
that night so he decided to carry salted nuts with him.
During the next two weeks he found himself eating a great
many salted nuts. In a way this was effective not only because it was punishment but also because with his mouth
full, Garth was less able to talk.

Unfortunately, as the weeks went by, Garth's target behavior that had decreased once again increased. Now Garth,
who kept careful charts and tabulations of the amount of
peanuts eaten, found himself more exhibitionistic than ever.
And he was eating more and more. After a month, much to
Garth's surprise, he had developed a distinct fondness for
salted nuts. What started as a punishment had become a
reward. No wonder then, that his targeted behavior increased instead of decreased.

Punishment is a many-sided tool to use to change our personalities. While it may appear an easy and straightforward way
of attacking an unwanted habit or action, it could turn out to
have all sorts of unpredictable effects. Kim was giving himself
shocks for sniffling and nail-biting, a plan which created a situation close to an avoidance-avoidance conflict (see Chapter Four).
Ultimately, like many others faced with several negative alterna-

tives, Kim just "left the field" by letting the battery run down and thereby extricating himself.

Punishment often motivates people to escape, as it did for Kim, rather than to change their conduct. The teacher who punishes a child for misconduct may find that child staying away from the classroom rather than being increasingly obedient. In the same way, when we punish ourselves for nail-biting, overeating, being too lazy or shy, we may find that we ourselves soon abandon our efforts. Punishment has not helped rid ourselves of undesirable actions but has driven us to get away from it all.

Another unwanted result of punishment is that it may paradoxically turn into a reward. Garth punished himself by forcing himself to eat peanuts. Soon however, he found a growing taste for salted nuts. Before too long, in fact, the nuts were a strong reinforcer so that his targeted behaviors increased, instead of decreased. What we think of as a punishment sometimes turns out to be a reinforcer so that we have to exercise extraordinary care in selecting punitive activities. Parents, and teachers particularly, often make the mistake of rewarding when they think they are punishing. An elementary teacher, for example was mystified by his inability to control a child's poor behavior.

> Mr. Sanford, a third grade teacher, complained that Clem was incurably inattentive. Nothing Mr. Sanford had done had resulted in the child consistently paying attention to his work. When the class was observed, it was found that there actually were very short periods when Clem did his work. But there were very many other periods when Clem looked around the room, talked to a neighbor, or walked about. Whenever Clem talked or looked around, Mr. Sanford walked over and scolded him to stick to his work. Since this punishment had failed, Mr. Sanford was advised to reverse the procedure. From now on he was not to attend to Clem in any way except for those short periods when he was actually working. Then he was to go over and say, "Good, you're doing very nicely."

Mr. Sanford believed he was punishing Clem's failure to do his schoolwork. Apparently, however, whenever Mr. Sanford came over to scold, Clem reacted positively to the attention he was getting. Just like the salted peanuts for Garth, the supposed scoldings for Clem eventually turned out to be reinforcers. All this teaches us a lesson. Within the limits of normal conduct, *almost any consequence you believe a punishment could actually turn out to be a reinforcer*. We, therefore, cannot provide a list of punishers. What is punishment for you in a particular situation, may turn out to be a reinforcer for someone else (or even yourself) in a different circumstance.

On the surface many kinds of consequences appear to be punishers. A mild electric shock, a scolding, going to bed early, skipping a meal and many other similar actions are sometimes effective punishment. But ultimately the only way to judge the validity of any supposed punisher is to watch closely whether or not it results in decreasing target behavior. Thus again, the necessity of keeping good records. Once you have chosen some behavior to eliminate, and selected what you believe a suitable punishment, record the behavior carefully. If the behavior continues to decline, you have chosen an effective punishment. But if the behavior remains the same, or even increases, your punishment is not working and it is time to rethink your plans for change and look for another approach.

With all we have said about punishment, still the most unwanted side effect is that it too often results in fear, anxiety, and other unpleasant emotions. Punishment may work, the spanked child may no longer question his parent's authority or directions, but he may also develop a gnawing fear of his own mother and father. In the same way, whenever we punish some of our own behavior, we may succeed in decreasing undesirable conduct but we may also make ourselves very uncomfortable and anxious about the entire situation. This was true in the case of a married man who found himself becoming sexually interested in one of his friends. Fearing the beginnings of an inclination towards homosexuality, he volunteered for an experimental program that administered strong electric shocks while presenting homosexual pictures and stimuli. The result was that this man developed a generalized serious anxiety about all sexual activities.

Punishment can help us change our behavior and personality but it is a very uncertain and potentially dangerous technique. Therefore, while we recommend punishment, we also warn that it be used with care and caution. When you want to change your personality by ridding yourself of specific behavior, first try the reinforcement techniques in Chapter Five and the other methods to be described later. If all else fails, consider punishment, but only as a last resort.

Incompatible Response

Instead of direct punishment, one of the best ways to eliminate behavior is to substitute a conflicting response. In the previous chapter, Mrs. Meyer wanted to eliminate her young son's eating with his fingers. She could, for example, simply have punished him directly by slapping his hands whenever he used them to pick up food. But she was wise enough to see that this might cause problems. Her child might become frightened of her or even refuse to eat at the table. So instead she chose to eliminate the finger eating habit by strengthening behavior that was incompatible with it. Whenever her son used a fork, spoon, and knife properly she complimented him. She reinforced responses that were in conflict with the undesired actions.

Mr. Sanford, the elementary school teacher, finally also made use of the principle of reinforcing an incompatible response to eliminate an unwanted behavior. He reinforced the inattentive child whenever he was paying attention. He rewarded the behavior opposite the undesired behavior and in this way slowly squeezed out the unwanted activities. In another instance a commuter complained that he was too cranky and tense and wanted to rid himself of these traits. Specifically he often came home tired, edgy, frustrated, and as a consequence, frequently argued with his wife, shouted at his children and otherwise ruined his dinner and evening. He tried punishing this behavior by delaying dinner whenever he exhibited anger but this only made the situation worse. With the help of a counselor an incompatible response was chosen.

Commuter: *What I need to do is get over that first hour at home. I need to unwind and feel human again so that I don't flare up so easily. . . Maybe I should drink more?*
Counselor: *No. No drinks. Have you tried punishing your outbursts?*
Commuter: *Yes, and it doesn't work! I need something else.*
Counselor: *We're going to try what we call an incompatible response. We're going to substitute some behavior for that hour*

or two of tension that is opposite, and reward that substitute behavior.

Commuter: *I like to go fishing. You want me to go fishing for an hour after I go home?*

Counselor: *Well, you say that humorously but it might not be a bad idea. If it were convenient and easy to do, it would be an excellent incompatible response because it has reward built right into it. But let's think of some other things you like to do in the evening. Tell me what you like. . .*

Commuter: *Well I like to eat, to drink, sleep, make love, shower and shave for the next day, read, watch T.V., talk, play bridge. . .*

After a thorough discussion of the commuter's likes and dislikes the counselor suggested the following plan. Immediately upon arriving home the commuter was to go to bed, nap or just rest for one half hour. Following this he was to shower and shave and lay out his clothes for the next day. Then he was permitted to join the family, have dinner and begin the evening. The new routine was a little difficult at first but soon it became habitual and totally eliminated the period of crankiness and irascibility following the commuter's arrival at home.

Notice that the incompatible response suggested to the commuter has "self-reinforcing" elements. The shower and shave following the nap is a reinforcement for the nap and is itself pleasurable. All the activities substituted for the undesired behavior are in and of themselves pleasant and desirable. But even if a nap and shower were emotionally neutral they would still be reinforcing. This is because they avoid the unpleasantness of a cranky argument. In other words, the incompatible response is often also a reinforcer just because it prevents the undesired behavior.

A very clear example of a substituted response being reinforcing was evident in the case of Dotty. She was a hairpuller. Whenever she was worried, puzzled or deep in a conversation she would pull her hair or pick at her scalp. This was a habit that was beginning to result in serious hair loss. In order to rid herself of this undesirable action, Dotty bought "worry beads" that she accidentally spotted in a store specializing in merchandise from the Middle East. Worry beads are plain or engraved wooden or stone beads strung together and made to be fingered or handled. Whenever Dotty felt the urge to scratch her head or pull hair she simply rubbed the beads instead.

In summary, in order to be rid of unwanted behavior, instead of punishing that activity, try substituting a response incompatible with the behavior. To help this incompatible-response method work for you, follow the rules suggested below.

1. Select a behavior that will be engaged in instead of the one you want to be rid of.
2. Make sure that the new response is desirable. Do not substitute one undesirable behavior for another. (Had the commuter been urged to drink to calm down, that would have been substituting one undesirable behavior for another.)
3. If possible, the new behavior should be reinforced even if it is self-reinforcing. (Dotty reinforced her use of the beads, instead of hair-pulling, by allowing herself to try new hairdos and accessories.)

Pay For Undesirable Behavior

If you cannot figure out any way whatsoever for ridding yourself of undesired conduct through introducing an "incompatible" response then you may have to try some form of punishment. So if you must punish, despite its possible complications, *try as a first step giving up some reinforcer* whenever the unwanted behavior occurs. Giving something up is punitive but is less likely to result in the potential difficulties of more direct punishment. To make this system work, think of some of the things you like that you would hate to give up. Put them in order from the easiest to do without, to something that you would deeply miss. Here are some reinforcers and activities that others have mentioned as very difficult to give up. These are not in any order but simply a random selection from the lists of several different persons.

drinking coffee	TV	golf
alcohol	telling dirty jokes	playing poker
clean house	fresh underwear daily	painting
sex	dyeing hair	pizza
gossiping	writing home	visiting
taking a drive	bird-watching	

The technique of paying for undesirable behavior by giving something up was used by Ralph, a graduate student in psychology. He was an exceptional tennis player and during summers earned considerable money working at a teenagers' camp as a tennis coach. Unfortunately his problem was that he was very "impatient," and when his students acted clumsily he became sarcastic and angered.

Ralph: *I try to hold my tongue but it doesn't work. When they don't follow my instructions I just get mad. . .I get exasperated, yell, call them jerks and worse. . .Some kid always ends up crying and that's not the way to coach. . .*

Counselor: *What have you done so far?*

Ralph: *I tried reinforcing, incompatible responses but I haven't come up with anything. I have got to stop this behavior. I'll lose the job eventually. But it is also a side of myself I do not want to reinforce. . .I know just the behavior I want to stop. I want to stop using sarcastic language and calling my students names. Then later I can learn to develop new behaviors. More patience and calm, an easy manner.*

Counselor: *Obviously the threat of eventually losing your job is not sufficient punishment. Otherwise you might have stopped.*

Ralph: *Right, that's right.*

Counselor: *Since you have tried various reinforcement procedures, then it might be worthwhile experimenting with some sort of punishment. Maybe we could start by thinking of something that you could deprive yourself of, immediately, everytime you are sarcastic and name call. . .*

Ralph: *I'm willing to try.*

Counselor: *Then think of something that you do every day that you really enjoy. Something that has real satisfaction for you.*

Ralph: *Well I love to eat. We could cut out lunch or dinner, or both.*

Counselor: *That's a potent reinforcer but I'm afraid that kind of deprivation might be self-defeating. You would get weak, be even crankier when you played and if we decided to skip supper you might just stuff yourself for lunch. We have to have some kind of deprivation that is complete. Something you*

*would really miss, yet is not a threat to your health or
functioning.*
Ralph: *Wait a minute. I've got it. I'll put my phone calls to
Maureen in the balance.*

Ralph had just become engaged to Maureen before he took
the summer job at camp. He eagerly looked forward to calling
Maureen, long distance, every night, and the two of them telling
each other the day's activities. Now Ralph decided that whenever
he treated his tennis students to his sarcasm he was not allowed
to call Maureen. Ralph explained his situation to Maureen and
she cooperated fully. Ralph kept careful records of his behavior.
During the first week he needed to punish himself nearly every
day. But as the weeks went by, his sarcasm consistently decreased
so that after twenty-six days he was able to call Maureen daily.

If you cannot think of anything to give up for an undesired
behavior try giving away money. But do *not* give the money to a
charity. Art was a chronic nail-biter and decided that every time
he bit his nails another dollar would go to the Salvation Army.
Before too long his records showed his nail-biting increasing.
Why? Simply because giving to the Salvation Army was reinforcing. It made Art feel good when he got the thank you notes and
thought about the work the Army was doing. Art's giving away
of money was not a punishment—it was a reward. To make
giving money away work, you must give it to something you distinctly do not like.

> Wilson was a business man who wanted to rid himself of his
> persistent overeating. After trying several different
> approaches he fined himself one dollar every time he
> overate or snacked between meals. At the end of the week
> all the money collected was donated to an ecology group
> that Wilson totally disagreed with. He did not like the
> group's aims or its methods and did not believe it should
> be allowed to function as a tax-free foundation trying to in-
> fluence the public and government. For Wilson, giving
> money to this group was significant self-punishment, and
> his overeating soon declined dramatically.

Giving money to a person, group, foundation or organ-
ization that you seriously disagree with or dislike can be an

effective self-punishment. We do not recommend simply throwing money away for that, too, can be indirectly reinforcing.

Direct Punishment

Direct punishment can work, as we have emphasized several times, but this method should be used only as a last resort because of the possibility of complications. We have several suggestions to help you use direct punishment most effectively in ridding yourself of unwanted behavior.

Punishment must occur every time, without exception, that the undesired behavior occurs. If you start making exceptions, skipping a punishment here and there, you are in effect teaching yourself to avoid punishment.

> Quentin was a very heavy drinker and was becoming worried that he might well become an alcoholic. With the help of his family physician, he was put on a medication called Antabuse in order to curb his drinking. Antabuse taken daily is in itself harmless, but when someone drinks in addition, the combination causes very severe cramps, vomiting and other serious symptoms. The effect is that the patient who has taken Antabuse cannot drink or he will be heavily punished by his body's reaction to the combination of Antabuse and alcohol.

Antabuse worked quite well for Quentin for the first two weeks but then he started forgetting his daily medication. He claimed that his lapses were due to his being too busy or that he just forgot about his daily treatment. Consequently since the punishment (actually threat of punishment in this case) was not total and continuous the drinking soon increased and the Antabuse program was eventually abandoned.

If punishment is to work it must be such that it can be applied every time and without fail to the undesired behavior. Any omission of punishment leaves an opening for the undesired behavior to strengthen itself and become even more difficult to eradicate. Therefore, when you choose a punishment, be certain that you can apply it with unvarying consistency. Here is a case of successful consistent punishment.

> Burton drove much too fast. He had several speeding tickets and was in danger of losing his license. Yet he still continually exceeded the speed limit. Finally he adopted a

punishment for eliminating his speeding. He kept a timer in his car that buzzed every five minutes. Whenever it buzzed he had to look at his speedometer. If Burton was over the posted speed limit he had to drop his speed ten miles below the limit and keep it that way until the next buzz. In this way Burton was forced to drive fairly slow every time he speeded. Burton continued this system religiously, without variation, and within the first month was driving within the posted limits nearly all the time.

Punishment through deprivation of a reinforcer may necessarily be delayed. When Ralph berated a tennis student he had to wait till evening for his punishment (not telephoning Maureen). Punishment that involves giving up something may take several hours to complete. But when direct punishment is tried, make sure that it is *immediate* and better yet *early*. We all know that delayed direct punishment can be worse than useless. The child threatened with a spanking when his father comes home may not be taught to rid himself of his undesired behavior. He may well be learning, however, to distrust his mother and fear his father. We also said that punishment should be early. We mean by this that as soon as the undesirable behavior begins, punishment should start. Do not wait for the behavior to complete itself and then punish. When behavior is allowed to finish then there is considerable likelihood of it being rewarding. The hair-puller who wants to stop her habit must punish as soon as she reaches for her hair and not after she has had the satisfaction of pulling for a while. The overeater must be punished immediately when he begins to raid the refrigerator, and not after he has reinforced himself with a delectable sandwich.

Both Brigitte and Harvey were overeaters and chose similar techniques for punishing themselves. Brigitte's plan was to follow eating too much food by taking an icy cold shower for five minutes. Harvey filled his bathtub with icy water and kept restocking it with ice cubes all day long. Whenever he started to feel he might be eating too much or made a move to get a between-meal snack, he went to the bathtub and stood in the icy water for five minutes. Brigitte allowed herself to be reinforced by the satisfaction of a full meal before punishing herself. Harvey in contrast punished himself as early as possible, before his undesirable behavior reinforced itself. As a result, Harvey was far more effective in curbing his overeating than Brigitte.

The same principle of punishing immediately and early finally helped a nineteen year old who was still a bedwetter. For most of his life he had continued to urinate in his sleep at least once or twice a month. After starting college his bedwetting increased till it happened every week. In the past this student had tried punishing himself by making himself wash the bedsheets and cleaning his room early the next morning but this and similar procedures had never worked very well. In addition to all their other failings these punishments were delayed and permitted the bedwetter the satisfaction of relief after his bladder was emptied. This individual, in order to be helped, needed to be punished immediately, and early, before the reinforcement of an empty bladder could be experienced. This student appeared at the college health clinic and was found medically normal. He was therefore instructed in the use of a Wee-Alert Buzzer, a system for controlling bedwetting marketed by Sears Roebuck and other firms. The Wee-Alert consists of a wired sheet connected to a buzzer. The sheet is placed on the mattress. A buzzer which wakes up the sleeper is activated when the sheet is wet by the first drops of urine. The sleeper still has a fairly full bladder and is now fully awake. In this instance, the Wee-Alert worked well. The punishment of a loud, sleep-disturbing buzz, plus a still full bladder quickly trained the nineteen-year-old student to control his urinary flow until he woke up in the morning.

Conclusion

Punishment can help us eliminate some undesirable personality characteristics but it must be used with great care. The unwise use of punishment could complicate our behavior by inducing fear, unpleasant emotion, and other undesirable side effects. If it is necessary to get rid of unwanted behavior, first try reinforcement with a response that is incompatible with the behavior. If this is not feasible, then unwanted actions can sometimes be extinguished by coupling them with giving up something. The personal reinforcer given up may be some habitual pleasure or money. If no other means seem available to stop the undesired behavior, then direct punishment may be tried. If an appropriate punishment is consistent, immediate and early, it can eliminate unwanted behavior.

Once punishment has worked to extinguish some undesirable trait or action, then one should remain alert for any reoccurrence and be ready to punish again. When an unwanted behavior has been thoroughly eliminated, new behaviors can grow, allowing our personality to change in the direction we have planned.

Seven
Controlling Fear and Worry

Many people would be content with their portion in life if only they were able to be less fearful and not worry quite so much. Most of us can easily think of ways in which our lives are narrowed and our potential dampened by all sorts of unreasonable anxieties. One person, worried about possible auto accidents, is afraid to sit behind the wheel and so never learns to drive. Another is so fearful of authority that he never manages to ask his boss for a well-deserved raise. Still others are afraid of sex, doctors, or flying, and as a consequence lose benefits and pleasures that others enjoy routinely.

What are your fears? How often and how intensively do inappropriate anxieties impair your life? Notice that we are talking about "inappropriate" worries. In many situations it makes sense to be concerned about safety, other people, or the unknown. But our fears are unwarranted when they bring about adverse emotional reactions to relatively ordinary events, consequently handicapping our lives. To get some idea of the extent to which normal adults have such exaggerated fears, over one hundred men and women were asked to list the events or things they truly feared. They were instructed to write down only those concerns that were serious enough to really interfere with their adjustment. The great majority of the participants recorded at least one fear. Only 20 percent said they were entirely free of irrational worries. The following is a selection among the fears mentioned most often. You can use this as a checklist to help you think about some of the potent anxieties that may be damaging your own personality.

People in authority	Insects
Dogs, animals	High places
Catching disease, germs	Crowds
Snakes, worms	Being looked at, watched
Guns, weapons	Crossing street
Going insane	Bats, birds
Doctors, dentists	Tests, examinations
Sex, nudity, opposite sex	Darkness
Cemeteries, death	Mice, rats
Funerals	Rejection, disapproval
Traveling	Injections, surgery
Public speaking	Handicapped people
Lightning, thunder	Cripples
Driving	Elevators, small spaces
Losing job, poverty	Death of loved one
Heart stopping	Loud noises
Dirt	Being hurt, assaulted
Police, jail	Movies

There is a way to control and reduce fear that all of us who have been parents or in similar positions have practiced. Imagine a young child, aged four, whom we take for the first time to a busy playground. The swings, seesaw and other apparatus fascinate him. But at the same time the screaming and running of so many children are frightening. Caring parents, aware of their child's fears, would introduce the new situation very slowly. Perhaps they would suggest that they sit on a nearby bench and just watch the excitement in the playground. The fearful child is now safe on the father's or mother's lap, feeling secure, warm, loved, and no longer afraid. At the same time, the child is learning about the playground. Perhaps as a next step, when the child is thoroughly comfortable watching from the safe distance of the bench, the parent takes him or her a little closer. And so it goes. Step by step the child moves closer and closer to participating in the playground while experiencing the security of being near the parent. Very likely, within a few hours the fearful child will be sufficiently confident to want to try the swings and seesaw.

The attentive parent has helped the child overcome anxieties about the playground by pairing good comforting feelings with an event that was feared. Notice that the parent did not force the child on a swing or seesaw. This would have destroyed the rapport, pleasure, and security that the child derived from the parental supports; it would have confronted the youngster with an overwhelming amount of anxiety in a very sudden and immediate way. Instead, the parent took small steps. When the child no longer feared watching from a distance, they moved closer. At each step forward the parent relied upon his or her presence to relieve the child's fear, using a technique that is called systematic desensitization. The parent was reconditioning: helping the child to lose anxiety through the pairing of pleasurable responses with fear responses.

Systematic Desensitization

Systematic desensitization is a fear-reducing method identified by psychiatrist Joseph Wolpe at Temple University. Wolpe induces a state of relaxation in his patients and then exposes them to a very weak anxiety-eliciting stimulus for a few moments. If the exposure is repeated several times, because it occurs in the presence of profound relaxation, it gradually loses its fear-producing properties. Then successively stronger fear stimuli are gradually introduced till each in turn loses its anxiety-potential.

The way in which this works can be seen from the history of a teenaged girl who was afraid of dogs. First she was instructed to carefully define and scale her phobia. The girl constructed a hierarchy of fears, from the least to the most anxious encounters with dogs. The situation the girl feared most was walking along the street and being confronted by a large, barking dog. She was least afraid of a very small, white, curly-haired dog while sitting in her aunt's living room. The client was trained in a series of exercises that would enable her to put herself into a state of total relaxation and tranquility. Now the teenager was ready to begin to decrease her anxiety. After she was completely relaxed, she was told to imagine the *least* frightening dog situation. Thus while she was in a state of near total calm she imagined herself in her aunt's living room with the tiny, white, curly-haired dog. After several sessions she was able to remain relaxed while visualizing this least frightening possibility, and was thus enabled to move up to the next most fear-producing situation.

From the above example it can be seen that systematic desensitization is a three-step procedure:

first—constructing a scale from the least to the most feared situation;
second—learning to relax completely;
third—presenting the fear situations during relaxation.

If we are to learn to overcome our own fears then we must follow this three-step procedure carefully and faithfully. None of the steps can be rushed nor can they be condensed. The first two steps should be practiced with patience and diligence before the introduction of the third, the fear situations.

Fear Hierarchy

Specify exactly what you are afraid of. If there is more than one situation or circumstance write them all down. The following is a list recorded by a thirty-four-year-old married woman:

1. I am afraid of going to football games. I don't like to be shoved and pushed.
2. I'm afraid of public toilets. I hate to touch door knobs.
3. I don't like to eat out. All that noise and commotion makes me very uneasy.
4. I get very upset if someone with a cold or something talks to me. I'm afraid they'll cough on me.
5. I'm afraid of catching diseases.
6. I'm afraid of waiting-rooms, like in a railroad station and places like that.

When you have written down all your fears you will notice that they fall into a pattern. The anxieties noted by the woman above were of two main kinds. First, she was afraid of crowds and, second, she feared catching a disease. Most people will have only one category of fear. That is they will be afraid of animals, or sickness, or small places, or abandonment, or unemployment. But a few individuals will have many different types of fears. They may be afraid of the opposite sex and afraid of talking to authorities, as well as afraid of being watched by others. It does not matter whether you have only one type of fear or several. As soon as you have specified your fear category you are ready to construct a hierarchy.

A fear hierarchy is built by writing down the least to the most feared situation in one category. You begin with a fear, real or imagined, that is least worrisome to you. Then you progress to the next worrisome fear in the same category until you have reached the most feared situation. It is usually best to have between ten and twenty hierarchical steps. The following is the fear hierarchy constructed by the woman who was afraid of disease. First she wrote down all her disease-related fears, each on a separate piece of paper.

Someone talking to me who has a cold.
Eating in a restaurant that doesn't look too clean.
Going to a public toilet.
The achy, fevery feeling that I'm coming down with
    something.
The doctor telling me I have some really bad disease.
Touching doorknobs.
Reading about some disease in the paper.
Hearing about some sickness on television.
Learning that a friend is sick.
Having to visit a sick person.
Having to care for a sick person.
The sight of a hospital.
People in wheelchairs or on crutches.
All the medicines and bottles and things in a drugstore.
Waiting in a doctor's office.
Handling money.

After you have written out all your fear situations you are ready to put them in hierarchical order. This means that you will put your fears on a scale with the least feared situation first, the next most feared situation second, and so on, until you reach the most feared condition. In sum, to construct a valid hierarchy, follow these instructions:

1. State the kind of thing that you are afraid of.
2. In a detailed way, describe specific situations, real or imagined, that you fear. (Review Chapter Two, on being specific.) List at least ten to as many as twenty fear circumstances, and write each on a separate sheet of paper.

3.   Arrange your anxiety situations in order from least to most frightening.

In the example above, the woman who was afraid of disease was able to record seventeen situations that she feared. She wrote each on a separate three-by-five-inch card so that she could arrange her fears into a hierarchy. Like many individuals, the woman with the sickness phobia found it convenient to work on a large table. She read through her pack of cards until she spotted the least feared circumstance, and put that at the left end of the table. Reading the cards again for her next-to-least feared situation, she put that to the right of the first card. She worked her way through all seventeen cards in this way. Occasionally she changed her mind and moved one card or another back or forward. When she finished, she reviewed the sequence again and again till she was certain that she had the right order. Here is the fear hierarchy that emerged.

1.   Reading about disease in the paper.
2.   Hearing about sickness on television.
3.   The sight of a hospital.
4.   People in wheelchairs or on crutches.
5.   Seeing all the medicines, bottles, and things in a drugstore.
6.   Touching doorknobs.
7.   Handling dirty paper money.
8.   Learning that a friend is sick.
9.   Waiting in a doctor's office.
10.   Eating in a restaurant that doesn't look too clean.
11.   Going to a public toilet.
12.   Having to visit a sick person.
13.   Someone who has a cold talking to me.
14.   Having to care for a sick person.
15.   The achy, fevery feeling that I'm coming down with something.
16.   The doctor telling me that I have some really bad disease.

Notice that this fear hierarchy may not agree with your own ordering of these specific situations. You might imagine that if you had a phobia about illness that you would put number twelve much further down and perhaps elevate number four. But this is not your list and the hierarchy you create for yourself may not be appropriate for anyone else. Remember therefore, when building your own anxiety hierarchy to arrange your fears in the order that you, personally, experience them. Do *not* try to create an order that you believe is a general, objective scaling of lowest to highest fears. Your list is for yourself alone and should describe only how you respond to your own fear situations.

The fear hierarchy for every person is different, even for those who are afraid of similar situations. Anxiety in heterosexual relations, for example, is common. Still, for each individual the hierarchy differs. The following is an illustration of the hierarchy constructed by a twenty-eight-year-old bachelor who was afraid of sexual relations. Notice that he needed twenty steps to reach his objective. This is because, over the course of years, his fears of sexual intimacy had increased to the point that even talking to a woman at a party caused him serious symptoms of anxiety such as perspiration, nausea, heart palpitations, and trembling. In contrast, many other persons with sexual fears have no anxiety in socializing. Here is the fear hierarchy that this man constructed.

1. Talking to a much older woman at work about some job thing.
2. Talking to the same woman and saying something personal like, "Nice day."
3. Eating in the cafeteria, and a woman I know is at the far end of the table.
4. Talking to a woman at the cafeteria table, but one who is too old or plain to be "eligible."
5. Talking personally for a short time to a nice-looking girl while at work.
6. Eating lunch with a nice-looking girl.
7. Walking with a nice-looking girl in the parking lot to our cars.
8. Being at a party and talking, disinterested-like, to a woman.
9. Being at a party and talking to a woman and we seem to like each other.
10. Asking a girl for a date.
11. Taking a girl out on a date.
12. Holding her hand or putting my arm around her crossing the street.
13. A friendly kiss and hug when I bring her home.

14. The girl inviting me in and I accept.
15. The girl sitting next to me close, and we are alone.
16. I kiss a girl.
17. I am touching a girl, caressing her, my hands are rubbing her body.
18. I touch a girl's breasts.
19. We touch each other's intimate parts.
20. We are undressing for intercourse.

When you have successfully created your anxiety scale you are ready to begin the next step in your fear-reduction program. Incidentally, the mere act of ordering your fears into a hierarchical sequence may have some anxiety-reducing benefits. Most people find that, after arranging their fears in succession, they are helped to see them in perspective. They can now understand that it is not all illness, all sex, all dogs, authority figures, or whatever they fear, but only certain situations.

Unconscious Fears   Unfortunately we are not always aware of all of our fears. In addition sometimes we may believe that we are afraid of situation X when what we really fear is situation Y, but are not conscious of it. For example, one woman believed that she was afraid of becoming pregnant. She constructed an excellent hierarchy of fears relating to pregnancy and then went on to the desensitization exercises. But somehow she did not make progress. After many weeks of work, her pregnancy anxiety had not diminished. The woman's continued lack of results necessitated some very careful examination of her motivation. Eventually it was revealed that she was not really afraid of pregnancy as such. What she did fear was the continuation of her marriage. Unconsciously she felt trapped in a frustrating marital situation and did not want to continue it. Her fear of pregnancy was merely an outer reflection of her true source of anxiety.

It is vitally important, therefore, that if we have any doubt about the validity of our anxiety, that we carefully examine our unconscious feelings. If we work on only the superficial manifestations of deeper worries, the chances of relieving our true anxieties are not very good. For instance, an older executive stated that he had an intense fear of speaking in public. This phobia greatly handicapped him in his work and he seemed highly motivated to rid himself of it. But though he labored diligently and followed all instructions, his success was very limited. Finally, with the help of a therapist, he reexamined his anxieties. To his surprise, his fear of public speaking turned out to be only a minor symptom of a much deeper and more pervasive worry. The executive grew up in a foster home and had been told that his natural mother had died hopelessly insane in a state institution. For all of his life this man had nursed a secret dread of becoming insane. His fear of public speaking was in actuality, a fear of saying something irrational, acting crazy, or in some way revealing that he was losing his mind. Once this man's true anxiety was uncovered he could work on it directly and clear up his related concerns like public speaking. As is evident from this and other biographies, it is important to scrutinize yourself very closely and be as certain as possible that your fear hierarchy is real and that it validly expresses the core of your feelings. Examine your own unconscious and be as certain as possible that no hidden anxieties lie behind the fears you consciously experience.

Relaxation

After you have constructed your anxiety hierarchy, lay it aside temporarily. Your objective now will be to learn to relax as totally as possible. You will bring your entire physical and psychological being into a state of calm and peacefulness that you have never experienced before. There are several methods for doing this but one of the surest is to systematically tense and relax particular muscles throughout your body. Here is the procedure.

1. Choose a quiet, private place with the lights dimmed. There should be a minimum of noise and no chance that you will be interrupted. Wear comfortable and loose clothing, take off your shoes and any constricting belts or jewelry and lie comfortably on your back on a soft mattress or pad. You may put pillows under your neck, head, arms, knees or arrange yourself in any manner that is maximally comfortable. Now relax, breathe slowly and evenly. Feel calm and content. Be prepared to stay about a half hour or more.
2. When you are lying comfortably, breathing peacefully, think

about your left hand. Feel its presence. Then, slowly, make a
fist. Then tighten your fist, make it very tight, concentrate all
your strength on your fist and feel the power in it. Then when
your fist is trembling with energy, slowly relax it. Let the
strength and tension drain away. Let the fingers open slowly.
Notice how that fist now feels increasingly free and calm. Let it
be totally tranquil. Let all the energy you devoted to tension
now devote itself to total peace. Tensing and relaxing your fist
will take a minute or two. Next do the same with your opposite
hand. Tense it to the maximum and then relax it.

Progressively work on every muscle group in your body.
You might go next to the powerful leg muscles, then the feet,
arms, chest, trunk, jaw, mouth, eyes, and finally your whole
head. In each case try to concentrate on that body part, feel it
becoming tense, energized, and powerful; then let all the
strength leave and relax. Finally your whole body will be
completely relaxed, deeply at peace and content.

3. Sometimes you may tense and relax a muscle group more
    than once to get the feeling of total composure. You may, for
    example, find it necessary to tense a foot muscle twice before
    you are completely satisfied with the relaxation you are
    getting. Or you may concentrate on relatively small muscles,
    perhaps getting best results working your way up slowly from
    the toes, to the ankles, to the foot, knee, calf, thigh, and so on.
    However you do your relaxation, be certain that you are satis-
    fied before you go further. When you have finished with your
    entire body, check it again. If you feel tension in any muscle or
    part, work on it again. By moving slowly and deliberately,
    your entire body will eventually be totally at peace.

4. This method of relaxation is sometimes helped by using a
    type of self-hypnotic technique. Some persons have taped their
    own voice telling them what to do. Then they play their tape
    for themselves and follow its instructions. Generally the time
    taken to relax will be longer at first and gradually shorten. The
    first few times it may take as much as forty-five minutes before
    you are convinced that you are tension free. As you get used to
    the technique, it may take less and less time so that ultimately
    ten to fifteen minutes will suffice to make you feel completely
    calm.

Desensitization

When you have satisfactorily written out your fear hierarchy and have become proficient at total relaxation, you are ready to begin desensitization. What you will be doing is pairing your specific anxiety situations with periods of relaxation. But this will have to be done very carefully. If, while relaxing, you suddenly recalled in vivid and gruesome detail one of your most frightening situations, this would destroy your mood of tranquility. For this reason when you put together a fear situation with relaxation you will begin by recalling the very least anxiety-provoking condition, that is, one at the bottom of your hierarchy. Here is how you should proceed.

1. Learn to relax completely. This may require as little as five or as many as twenty practice sessions. When you are ready to begin your first actual desensitization, begin by studying the sentence you have written describing your least feared situation. Remember that situation but do not dwell upon it. Instead clear your mind, go to your usual private spot and get yourself completely relaxed. Relax totally, feel perfectly at ease before going to the second step.

2. After you are perfectly relaxed, start thinking about your fear, the one that is the lowest on the hierarchy. If you still feel relaxed, think about your fear in some detail. Construct the situation in your mind so that you see the faces of the people, the room they are in. Imagine all the particulars of your fear. *But*, if your thinking about your fear has made you lose some of your good relaxed feeling, *stop!* Let the fear leave your mind. Focus again on relaxation. You can always return to your fear later on. Right now you have to feel calm and peaceful again. *The point of desensitization is to permit you to vividly imagine your fear, and still feel relaxed and unworried.*

3. When you are able to clearly imagine the first hierarchical fear and still remain totally calm, you are ready to go on. You may require only one session before you are ready to proceed. Most people, however, are well advised to try several separate couplings of relaxation with the fear that is the first in the hierarchy. When you are completely convinced that you can do both together, go on to the next anxiety. Again relax com-

pletely, imagine the first fear that you have already "conquered," pause and start your second hierarchical fear. If, while thinking about the second fear, your relaxation is disturbed, stop the fear and work again on your relaxation.

To review, the procedure will always be to associate the fear with relaxation. Whenever you are able to be completely relaxed while imagining a specific level of fear you will move up to the next higher anxiety. Gradually you will be able to visualize in surprisingly realistic and dramatic detail the top of your anxiety hierarchy without losing your relaxation. You will be able to think of the most fearsome situation in your repertoire and still be calm. What you will have done is disarmed your own anxiety. You will have learned to control and reduce the stimuli that have been provoking all those worrisome emotions.

The process of pairing a fear situation with relaxation is a delicate and subtle exercise requiring a high degree of awareness and sensitivity. You need to free your imagination, to be alert to your body and to be prepared to put forth considerable energy. The following is a good illustration of an individual who worked diligently and effectively. This is the twenty-eight-year-old man who had a sex phobia. He was asked to tape-record his recollections after each of his sessions. It usually took him three to five sessions before he was able to move up from one to the next in his fear hierarchy. After forty-seven desensitization trials he had worked his way up to number 15 in his hierarchy—sitting alone with his date in her living room. Here is part of his description of his forty-eighth desensitization experience.

Again I got myself completely relaxed. It only takes me about five minutes now. I get each muscle calm, at peace. My breathing is slow. I feel very good. Very loose like I'm floating. No cares. My whole body feels good. It's time to concentrate. I review number 14. She's invited me in and I accept. I have that one licked. I'm very calm so it's time to move up my hierarchy. Pam and I are sitting on her couch. In her living room. The lights are low. I look at her. She is wearing something like a halter top. Her breasts are small, I think. But you can see the curve of her breast through her top. My imagination is very vivid today. I sense the scene very clearly and I also sense that I'm losing some of my relaxation. I stop the scene. I make my mind a blank again and I can feel a little tension in my body. I think it is my neck, maybe. And it could be my trunk. I think about my neck. I tense it, relax it. I go through the whole procedure with my neck, my trunk, whatever else I think is making me feel tense. The scene has left me. Just my body now that I will relax again.

When I am completely relaxed, I go back to thinking about Pam. She is sitting very close, on the couch. We are sort of half-turned to each other. She is smiling and talking about the movie we saw. I can smell her perfume. She smells so fresh and clean. I still feel relaxed. I go further. I imagine myself looking at her skirt and her body. Her skirt is high on her leg. I can see her thigh. I can see how her hips press against the skirt. I can see the line made by her upper leg. I can see her waist, the faint outline of her stomach. I feel my relaxation slipping away again. I stop the fantasy and concentrate again on getting my body to relax.

This man with sexual fears makes his anxiety situations as realistic as possible. He thinks not only of a girl, but of a particular one. He imagines as many details as possible about his situation. And as soon as he feels himself becoming anxious he stops his fantasy and concentrates again on relaxation. In his desensitization, as he went higher and higher in his anxiety hierarchy, he needed to employ progressively more relaxation sessions for each fear situation before going further. In this particular instance, sitting on a couch alone with his girl friend, he required six trials before he could imagine it in the most intimate detail and still remain free of fear.

There are several hints that will help assure the success of desensitization. They are as follows:

Always spend at least one session on each hierarchical fear before going on to the next. There is no hurry and if you have the least doubt spend two or more sessions on a specific fear.

Never, ever, go on to the next fear until you are absolutely certain you can imagine the current fear and still be completely relaxed. In fact, always begin successive desensitization trials with the last fear that you believe you have already "mastered." This is a check, enabling you to make sure you have overcome that fear; it also prepares you to move up your anxiety scale.

During desensitization, whenever you feel that a fear image

is too frightening, that you are losing your composure, stop. Concentrate again on relaxing. Make sure you are completely calm before you go back to the fear.

Neither be impatient nor discouraged. Take your time. Some few people seem to breeze through an entire anxiety hierarchy with little more than a dozen trials while others require as many as a hundred. There is no rush; speed is not a requirement. Work at your own pace, be alert to your needs, and know that your efforts assure a good likelihood of success.

Results

When you have successfully completed the desensitization series you will feel a new freedom from worry and anxiety. You will *not* be ready to enter a lion's cage, instantly confront your boss, lose every inhibition, or immediately overcome your every worst fear. But you will be able to begin to handle in real life what you have already experienced in fantasy. The imaginary coupling of your fears with relaxation will have removed much of the emotional barrier that stopped you from even attempting to deal with your anxieties. Now you will be ready to try with confidence those experiences that previously were too frightening to consider.

The desensitization procedure not only removes anxiety blocks but also serves as a model demonstrating the path and pace needed to conquer any remaining fears. When you constructed a fear hierarchy you learned to move ahead slowly and gradually. During desensitization you *imagined* a step in the hierarchy and stayed at that level till you were able to feel relaxed. In the same way now, in real life, you will *try* a situation in your fear hierarchy, and try it again and again, until you feel completely comfortable. Then you will move a step higher, repeat that again and again, till once more you feel secure. How this works can be seen by reading the diary of the woman who was afraid of disease. She had worked very conscientiously on desensitization and in little more than a month had successfully moved through her entire fear hierarchy. Then she put her new learning into practice. She kept a daily journal and here are some excerpts.

June 6:   Today, after only thirty-eight days I have finished desensitization. For the third time I have visualized my very worst fear, being told I was very sick, and I remained calm. Now I am ready to see the results.

June 7:   Today I started my real-life experiment to see if I am as free of fear as I think I am. I started with number five on my hierarchy, visiting a drugstore. I thought that felt about right. I know I have no difficulty any more with anything lower. I visited the Rite-Aid store and I felt fine. No problems at all.

June 12:   Still no problems. I handled lots of paper money today. The dirtier, the better, and I feel fine. But I will go slowly, I don't want to rush and lose my confidence.

June 25:   This is the third day that I have been visiting sick people. I am still not completely at ease. I still feel some twinge. Tonight I will desensitize again, and repeat the visit tomorrow. I will continue this till I feel completely comfortable.

Most people, after finishing their desensitization trials, put their new fearlessness to the test by starting relatively low in their hierarchy. They try out their third or fourth fear and usually find themselves comfortable and at ease. Then, as they work their way up the hierarchy, they make sure they feel entirely secure before moving on. Occasionally, if they seem to hit a block, feel some of their old anxieties returning, they repeat a desensitization session. This was done several times by the woman with the disease phobia. When she noticed her uneasiness in visiting a sick friend, for example, she relived this event in fantasy, while thoroughly relaxed. She continued alternating such desensitization trials with trips to see her sick friends until the actual visits became anxiety free. In this same way, though your own patient movement up the fear hierarchy, pausing, repeating and desensitizing whenever necessary, you will eventually find yourself surprisingly comfortable in situations you once dreaded.

Conclusion

Desensitization is a potent tool that can help overcome nearly any worry. Clearly describing each phobic situation and constructing a scale of anxiety is the first step. Next you learn to relax fully and totally. Finally you systematically couple each fear with profound relaxation, thus gradually diminishing your anxiety. After desensitizing an entire hierarchy of fear in your imagination and with your body, you will be able to successfully work on those same situations in real life.

The desensitization procedure, just like any other self-learning experience, is not without problems. Some persons will find it hard to imagine their fear situations with sufficient intensity. Others may experience trouble turning their anxiety images "on" and "off." A few may have difficulty ferreting out their actual fears since some of their anxieties may be deeply unconscious. All of this is to say that an occasional obstacle can be expected by most individuals. But in nearly all instances these detours are overcome just by a little more effort and a little more practice. In those few instances when anxieties appear difficult to control, or in those rare cases when desensitization techniques seem to make things worse, professional help should be sought.

Eight
Fantasy
and
Role
Playing

In systematic desensitization (Chapter Seven), we used fantasy combined with relaxation to help us overcome fear. Now we will use fantasy to reach our goals directly. We will help ourselves change by imagining we are the person we want to be or that we are doing the things we want to do. Another method is role playing, which is a fantasy that is acted out, to achieve our ambitions. We will set up imaginary situations and with the help of others act out parts we want to play in real life.

To see how fantasy works, here is the case of George. He is twenty-six years old and has never had what he calls a "real" job. Since dropping out of college he helped out, part-time, in his father's dry cleaning store. His father was only able to pay him fifty dollars a week, and this meant George continued to live at home. George feels he is too dependent and shy. He has defined his goals in behavioral terms and concluded that his biggest handicap has been his inability to face job-hunting and particularly the personnel interview. To overcome this barrier he has recently taken a night-school course on how to find a job. Besides learning to dress, write a resumé, and fill out an application, he learned to prepare for the interview through fantasy. Here is a segment of his fantasy. All of the following is taking place in George's mind.

Boss: *I want a go-getter in this job. Not the kind satisfied with $50 a week that you were making at the store. Are you a go-getter?*

George: *Well sir, I was younger then. I have learned now what I want in life. I want to work hard and make something of myself.*

Boss: *Why did you drop out of college?*

George: *I dropped out because it wasn't leading me anywhere. I am not putting down the value of education. I had some courses that were really good but they were preparing me for being a teacher and I found out that's not for me. I belong in the business world where you compete for every dollar you make.*

Boss: *What do you think would be a fair salary for you?*

George: *Well, frankly I haven't given that much thought. I want to be paid just about as much as anyone else with my background in the company—that's starting out of course. But I think more important than my salary is knowing whether or not I have lots of room to go on up. I mean I don't mind starting low but I want to know that if I really do a good job I will be well rewarded for it.*

In his fantasy George was very harsh with himself. He pictured the interviewer as an extremely probing individual. In actuality most job interviewers are far more casual. In order to round out his experience George therefore role-played the job interview. He asked a friend to imagine he was an employer interested in hiring George. The friend was given George's resumé and told to imagine a specific job opening in his company.

Friend (Boss):   *I see on your resume that you're a skier. Where do you ski in winter?*

George: *Mainly upstate. I guess I don't travel very far. I'm just interested in good skiing. Nothing too fancy.*

Friend (Boss):   *Uh huh. Are you pretty active in sports? I mean do you do other things as well?*

George: *Well, I bowl a little. Sometimes I hike and mainly I guess in summer I swim. I try to keep active and stay in shape.*

Friend (Boss):   *Well, we like young people here that stay active. It keeps them healthy. What makes you interested in this job? The one you're applying for?*

George: *Well, I have always wanted to work in the electronics industry. It has seemed to me that every new development, computers and optical-scanners and all those, are the result of the work that companies like this are doing. I mean it is an opportunity to share in the growth of technology and of business at the same time.*

Friend (Boss):   *Do you think you can work with people from many different backgrounds, engineers, salesmen, physicists, assembly workers, and the like? What's your feeling about that?*

George: *Well, I think that's one of the really good things about this kind of job. You're not just working with other people all of whom are salesmen, or accountants and that. You rub elbows with all sorts of different points of view.*

Notice how much more realistic George's friend is in simulating an actual interview. Frequently we are harder on ourselves in fantasy than real life actually is. Ultimately, through both his role playing and his fantasy, George enabled himself to meet a challenge he once considered impossible. He had several successful interviews and was offered a job.

Fantasy and role playing can be used to bring about all sorts of personality changes. Both techniques together, or either one alone, may help you learn such different things as interviewing for a job, overcoming sexual inhibition, or curbing the amount you eat. Let's begin by looking at fantasy a little more closely to see how it can be put to work for us.

Fantasy

The last two centuries in the Western world have been the ages of Reason and Science. Fantasy, daydreams, imagination, and similar reverie have been called wishful thinking and have been relegated to children and neurotics. In this technological age that so emphatically values the real and concrete, fantasy has been made to seem irrelevant, even harmful. Certainly an individual who lives entirely in an imaginary universe is likely to be in need of treatment. But there is a valuable place for fantasy in the lives of healthy men and women.

In a classic study reported by John Oxendine in his book, *A*

Psychology of Motor Learning (Appleton-Century-Crofts, 1968), high school students roughly equal in basketball-playing ability were divided into three groups. The first group went regularly to a basketball court for several weeks to practice shooting. The second group was instructed to *imagine* themselves shooting. They did not go to the courts but fantasized practicing as often as the first team actually practiced. The third group of high school students did nothing.

After several weeks all three groups were brought to the basketball court to play, and their performances were compared. The group that actually practiced did quite well. The third group that did nothing did very poorly. Nothing startling so far. But what was extremely impressive was that the group of students who only imagined they were practicing did better than the no-activity group, and almost as well as the actual players. The group that played the game in *fantasy actually improved their basketball skills.* Subsequent research by many other investigators has demonstrated that similar mental rehearsal of sports activity can visibly increase actual performance. In fact, some coaches now believe that practice that is half mental and half physical may well be more effective than purely physical practice alone.

All of us have doubtlessly used fantasy, daydreaming and the like all our lives but have never realized its potential. Perhaps we have even been ashamed of our own tendency to be imaginative, or maybe we have simply not known the power that our fantasy possesses. Fantasy can help us change if we know how to enlist it in our service. There are several ways in which imagination can help but one of the easiest is to visualize several different scenarios. Starting with an actual personal problem, we imagine several different ways in which it could be solved. We become playwrights, using our own life situation to create different scenes. Here is an example. Roberta was a twenty-eight-year-old divorcee. Since she had married very young, at seventeen, she had had almost no dating experience. She had been divorced for nearly a year and had not accepted a single invitation to go out with a man. She did have a few offers but was so uncertain that she turned down all the men that approached her.

Roberta: *I know it sounds silly, but I just feel so awkward. I dont't know how to behave or what to talk about, or if they seem more than casually interested, what to do. I wouldn't mind a sexual relationship but I definitely do not want to get serious. I just want to date for fun.*

Counselor: *I'm going to ask you to be a playwright. Imagine several different scenes all dealing with a first date. Imagine what you would say, what the other person would say, and so forth. Fill in everything, like how and where you meet, where you go, and all details. Be specific, that is, use real people in the cast. Think what everyone actually says and does.*

Roberta took her instructions home with her and was asked to come back with at least three different date scenes. Each was to be a total fantasy, yet realistic enough to have actually happened to her. Here are excerpts from two of the scenarios that Roberta created.

A physician where Roberta works, Dr. Baum, has hinted again at a date. He said, "Have you seen *Timothy Fairweatherr, '49* playing at the Academy?" So, this time, instead of ignoring him, I said that I hadn't seen the film but was hoping to. So he said maybe we could go together after work. And I said, "Great." After work he suggested we eat first so we drove to the new Japanese place. When we got there it was crowded so we had to wait. Jeff (Dr. Baum) had not said much, so I began talking. "Japanese food is not strange to me. They eat a great deal of fish, some squid and octopus too." Jeff said, "Well it does sound a little different, you must admit." I agreed and told him, "My father was in the navy and spent a lot of time in Japan. He would bring back ingredients and cook things wrapped in seaweed, or make a sauce to go with little slices of raw fish. It was really very good. I like it. Jeff asked if this restaurant served those real Japanese things and I told him I suspected this was a very Americanized place."

During the party we got into a corner and we began talking about my marriage. I had brought it up, I guess, by asking Jeff if he had been married. I was explaining the good things and bad about my own marriage. "I liked Bill, I still do, a lot. He can be very kind and very gentlemanly. But he is also very overwhelming. He wanted to control everything about me, and he was fiercely jealous." Jeff asked, "Well did you give him reason to be?"

Roberta's scenarios are detailed and complete, as they should be. She does not just say, "We'll go to dinner and talk about Japanese food," or "At a party we'll talk about marriage."

In her fantasy she created the actual dialogue. She described exactly what she said and what her companion said. In still another fantasy Roberta imagined herself starting an affair with an older man who lives in her apartment house. She frequently saw him on the elevator and they usually just exchanged pleasant greetings. She found him very attractive but did not know how to indicate her interest.

In real life Roberta felt too "shy" to "pick up" the older man. But in her fantasy she was able to make contact with him. She was direct, open, and self-confident in her imagination.

Roberta: *(As she rides up the elevator with the man.) I notice that you always seem to carry a bulging briefcase. I guess you must be a lawyer or accountant or someone with a lot of paperwork.*

Man: *Not really. I am an editor. I work for a publishing house.*

Roberta: *Oh that's fascinating. That must be very exciting. You know I read a lot and I would love to talk with you about writing.*

Man: *Well that would be nice.*

Roberta: *Why don't you stop by sometime. I live in 8-C. Where are you?*

Counselor: *That sounds like a good fantasy, Roberta. You are not as shy and you are straightforward as you want to be. But what would you have said if he had answered that he was a lawyer or a research chemist.*

Roberta: *I was prepared for almost anything except an undertaker! If he had said "lawyer" I would have said that I could use some legal advice, or accounting help. If he had said "chemist" I would have said pretty much the same; that it was fascinating and I would like to have a chance to hear more about it. I practiced an answer for nearly every profession. I even had something ready if he refused to say what he was.*

Counselor: *What?*

Roberta: *I would have said, "I enjoy a challenge. Could I guess what kind of work you do? Could you stop by at my place sometime (I'm in 8-C), and give me a few minutes and a couple of questions so I could take a real guess?*

Just as fantasy can help us *do* something it may also be useful in helping us *not* to do something. Perhaps we want to eat a little less, cut down on how much we smoke or drink or otherwise lessen or eliminate some undesirable habit. Very often, freely imagining the potential consequences of our unwanted behavior will bring about the changes we want. To use fantasy to help you to stop doing something, follow this procedure.

1. First imagine the behavior you want to be rid of. But think about it favorably. Imagine lighting up a cigarette after a heavy meal, or biting your nails, or eating too much. Picture your undesired characteristic as positively as possible.
2. You should create such an inviting fantasy about your undesired behavior, that you feel tempted to do it. But you won't. Instead you will follow your positive ,fantasy with as horrid and exaggerated an image as possible of the consequences of your actions. For example, if you want to cut down on drinking, after you have the favorable picture, next imagine yourself a down-and-out thoroughly addicted and debilitated alcoholic lying in an alleyway!
3. After you have thoroughly frightened yourself, stop the image. Now imagine yourself back in the original situation. But now you decline a second drink, or a third helping of pie, or an eleventh cigarette. Now you fantasize how your moderation makes you healthy, desirable, and master of your own destiny.

In the examples above, we are not asserting that drinking, smoking, and other such emotionally-charged behaviors are eliminated through fantasy. Fantasy is not likely to cure an alcoholic or curb a compulsive four-pack-a-day smoker. But for most nonaddicted people, fantasy can be a useful way to cut down on many undesirable behaviors ranging from excessive spending to eating (see Chapter Nine).

Fantasy may also help us get completely rid of minor but annoying habits. Such things as nail-biting, chewing the ends of pencils, playing with one's hair, nose picking, head scratching, and similar mannerisms can frequently be eliminated through fantasy. Here is a recommended method followed by Myrna. She worked as a teller in a bank and sat at her window for long periods with nothing to do. Almost always, whenever her hands were not busy, she played with her hair. She ran her fingers through her hair, pulled at strands, curled her locks and sometimes scratched her head. This is her description.

A long time ago I saw a film about mental hospitals. I remember a woman sitting sort of alone, lonely, on a wooden bench. She wore sort of a white hospital smock. She looked terrible. And she was pulling at her hair. I think she had already pulled a lot of it out. That was the picture that I knew I would use in my fantasy. It's horrible.

I began thinking of my window in the bank. I was sitting waiting. I was playing with my hair. It felt good. I uncurled it. I let it roll back. I saw just what I was doing. I fantasized it all in detail. I like my hair.

Then when I felt really good about it, and was really into hair pulling, I switched fantasies. I saw myself pulling my hair more and more. I saw how I was becoming more and more peculiar. Everybody was beginning to look at me in the bank. Then, God, my hair was starting to come out in my hands. In bunches! It was terrible. I was getting really weird. I was picking at my head. I couldn't leave my hair alone. I was going crazy. This terrible picture of that poor woman in the hospital. That was me. I had lost my senses. I couldn't stop.

I let that fantasy go on till I really shuddered. It was very real. Then I stopped. I relaxed and I tried to get back the bank picture. All is calm. I am waiting for another customer. Nothing to do. I do not tease my hair. My hands are in my lap. I feel very good. I feel very superior to that woman in the hospital. I feel no urge to touch my hair. I like myself now. People admire me. My hair is beautiful, so natural. I feel very good.

When we use fantasy to help rid ourselves of some behaviors it is usually wise to go very slowly. We should work on eliminating the undesirable habit in very small stages. Myrna's first objective was to omit head scratching for only one morning per week. Thus on a Monday morning before going to work she spent a half hour fantasizing the consequences of continual head scratching. She promised herself that if she got through Monday morning she would not fantasize and could scratch as much as she pleased the rest of the week. Each week, however, Myrna added another morning. During the second week, for example, she fantasized forbidding herself scratching for both Monday and Tuesday mornings. Eventually Myrna worked her way gradually through the entire week, and from scratching up to pulling. In this slow and patient way she got rid of her hair pulling entirely.

Reinforcement

We do not have to rely on fantasy alone to change our behavior. Now that we are familiar with reinforcement (see Chapter Five), we can use these procedures along with fantasy. Myrna the hair puller, used both fantasy (visualizing horrible consequences) and reinforcement to stop her habit. Her reinforcer was the habit itself. She permitted herself unlimited hair teasing if she successfully completed a stipulated period without pulling. The Roberta who had trouble socializing with men also used a reinforcer together with fantasy. She fantasized different ways in which she might get to know the older man on the elevator. But she also promised herself a reward if she actually put one of her fantasies into operation. As soon as she actually invited the man to her apartment, she promised she would buy herself an expensive leather bag that she wouldn't have otherwise bought. In psychological terms, Myrna's reinforcer was internal and Roberta's external.

Fantasy that is reinforced internally draws its reward from the imaginary or behavioral process itself. Internal reinforcement is particularly valuable when we want to rid ourselves of some habit. Like Myrna, we visulaize the potential unpleasant results of our fantasy but also reward ourselves by engaging in the undesired action under certain conditions. If we do not pull our hair, overeat, or chew our nails on Sunday, Monday, and Tuesday, then we are free to do these things on other days.

Of course when the undesired behavior is itself used as the reinforcer, the reward becomes scarcer and scarcer. Soon as a matter of fact, the bad habit loses it reinforcing properties, and this is as it should be. Myrna, for instance, found that after she had eliminated hair pulling on all mornings she seemed somehow not to pull her hair very much during afternoons either. Gradually even without explicitly planning it, she no longer pulled her hair, even during periods when it was permissible.

The less and less Myrna pulled her hair, the more

momentum her new personality gained. She put it, "All of a sudden I had the feeling, 'I can really do it.' I felt proud of myself." Myrna experienced the satisfaction of seeing something actually happen that she hoped for and fantasized about. This inner feeling of pride and joy was similarly reported by Roberta. One of Roberta's problems was that she felt shy. She did not want to accept a date because it meant she would have to talk about herself. To overcome her shyness, to be more outgoing and open, Roberta fantasized all sorts of conversations with Dr. Baum. In these talks she freely described her own background. But could she do this in real life? Would her "shyness" not make her tongue-tied once the situation actually occurred? The answer to both questions was no. Roberta's many fantasy-scenarios made the situation so familiar that she found it easy to begin. Once started, the rewarding satisfaction of socializing with men encouraged her to continue. Roberta described it:

> I had fantasized so many dramas about dating Jeff and talking to him. I had all sorts of mental conversations with him that I had never had with anybody. That I just could never have had because I was so shy.
>
> We did finally get together and we did go for dinner. He said something about getting to know me better and I just started talking. It was all so familiar. As if I had done this so often before that it just seemed so natural. And then the thing was that I had this real feeling of satisfaction. I felt proud of myself. I said, "Roberta, old girl, you can do it, we're proud of you." It really went so well.

When we finally do something that we have systematically fantasized, the doing of it is internally reinforcing. Now we know that we can actually change in the way we have previously only dreamt about. Inside we are warmed and rewarded by our own feeling of pride and success.

If internal reinforcement, that satisfying inner glow, is not enough, we can add external reinforcers to our fantasy. If we actually do what we have imagined ourselves doing, we can give ourselves a prize. Roberta promised herself a handbag for starting a conversation with the older man. Another individual might choose a new stereo, theatre tickets, or some other luxury or extravagance. A very special and potent kind of external reinforcement can be obtained through one's friends. Here is Andrew describing how he used a friend as a reinforcer.

> Roz knew how much I wanted to be the singer in the group. But she also knew my feelings of inadequacy. I was so self-defeating in my head and I wanted to change. After I began doing this in fantasy, I told Roz about it. She was waiting to see what would happen. I think she was skeptical of how much fantasy would help me feel the confidence I needed to get up and be the singer.
>
> When I did it I had the feeling I was doing it for Roz. She would be proud of me, and she was when I told her. She gave me a lot of reinforcement. The way I see it now is that fantasy primed the pump. And the reinforcement Roz gave kept me going.

The praise of others can be an excellent reinforcer. Often it is far more effective than promising ourselves a material treat. Consequently whenever we combine fantasy with a social reinforcer (someone else's praise) we are likely to make very rapid progress. But one needs to be very careful to select the right friend. It is little use sharing our project with someone who is indifferent, callous, or even hostile. If Andrew had selected a certain musician friend, he might not have gotten praise for his effort to sing, but criticism instead. Be sure that you look for social reinforcement only from a person who is positively interested in you. Pick a friend who is understanding and supportive, and as pleased about your triumphs as you are.

Role Playing

When we role play we act out fantasy. Perhaps we want to ask our boss for a raise. We have fantasized several different scenarios. But we are still uncertain. How might the boss react and how will we feel about his responses? One way of finding out is to role play. We ask a friend to help, and assign him a role. Today he is a grumpy and stingy boss and is to react negatively to our raise request. Next, he will play the role of a sympathetic boss but one who wants us to prove our work merits a raise. Role playing is an intermediate step between pure fantasy and hard actuality. The following describes three special ways in which role playing can help to bring about personality change.

Coping   Fantasy is an excellent way to learn to cope with new situations. But, occasionally, our fantasized scenarios go just so far. We are not really able to imagine *all* possible situations and contingencies. Our mind is limited and it would be nice if in some way we could extend the range of our mental images. This can be done through role playing. In the example of the employee who wanted a raise the worker feared that his boss might react in ways he had not imagined. Therefore he asked several friends to play the role of the boss. In this way the employee could learn to cope with all sorts of unexpected responses that his boss might give him. As an illustration of just how role playing can help us learn to cope with situations never envisioned in our fantasy, here is what actually happened to the man who role played asking for a raise.

> I had two different friends role play the boss and both were very good, although I didn't really encounter anything new from them. I had already pretty much fantasized all the kinds of things they were saying. But then I asked another friend, Jay, to role play. I didn't tell Jay anything, such as to be grumpy, or skeptical or anything. I just asked Jay to role play a boss and I was going to ask him for a raise.
>
> Jay pulled a real surprise. After I asked him for a raise, he said that it was a worthwhile request and that I was a good worker. But he also said that they were thinking of cutting down on my department and about letting me go. He put me in the situation where I had to prove that I was worth keeping. I really sweated but I finally came up with enough arguments to keep me from getting laid off.

In the instance above, the employee learned to cope with a situation that he had never imagined. Through role playing his fantasy was extended to include the threat of being without a job. Through role playing the worker was able to work out several new scenarios which ultimately enabled him to face his boss successfully.

Discovery   Closely related to learning to cope with new, unimagined situations, role playing often lets us discover new feelings and behaviors. In our fantasy we are often fairly unoriginal about ourselves. We tend to rely on old habits and at best visualize our changed personality in a very narrow way. Through actual role playing, however, we may uncover aspects of our personality that we were totally unaware of. An amusing instance of this occurred in a group of students who were learning to role play. A college senior felt that she was too passive and dependent. She believed that she was always at the receiving end of all heterosexual relationships and she wanted to learn to be more assertive. Specifically, in behavioral terms, she wanted to be able to break off a relationship when she felt it was no longer interesting to her. She asked to role play a young woman who was going to tell her boy friend she no longer wanted to see him. Another student volunteered to be the boy friend and he was told to be clinging. He was to resist breaking off the relationship.

Girl: *I think we've been together just about a whole year now.*

Boy: *Yeah, It's been great.*

Girl: *Yes it has been but I also think we've not made any new friends at all. We even seem to have lost some of our old ones.*

Boy: *Well that doesn't matter since we have each other.*

Girl: *That is nice but we should have other friends too, don't you think?*

Boy: *Not really. I'm very satisfied just the two of us being together.*

Girl: *Well that is nice but I think I like knowing more people. I mean we should be friends, too, but I feel I want to experience more.*

Boy: *You mean you want to go out with other guys, is that it?*

Girl: *Well, I mean, we have been seeing only each other—*

Boy: *I don't know what you're trying to say. But I feel very strongly about you. I thought we had this thing going now that is going to be permanent. We love each other. Don't we? I love you. I want to marry you.*

Girl: *You do! Oh my goodness! Really? Well sure! Let's get married!*

The girl was totally surprised at her reaction. She had never consciously contemplated marrying any of the several males with whom she had had a close relationship in her college years. She believed that her problem was being too dependent. She thought she wanted more freedom, to play the field, to be a "swinging single," and she hoped to learn some of this through role playing.

Instead she discovered, much to her surprise, and to the amusement of the rest of the group looking on, that she enthusiastically accepted the idea of marriage.

When we role play we go outside of the limits that our own fantasy has imposed. After all, even our unfettered imagination is limited. Role playing taps the fantasy of someone else. Their personality and behavior can call forth all sorts of traits inside of us that we may not know we possess.

Consequences Another very valuable contribution that role playing can make is to help us learn consequences. Sometimes it is difficult to imagine unpleasant situations or results. In the same student group as the one mentioned above, a nineteen-year-old sophomore felt that he was on the way to becoming very overweight. He recognized that he simply overate and wanted to be able to cut down. To help motivate more careful eating habits, he asked to role play an obese young man on a date. The girl who played the date was told that she was to treat the student as if he were very fat. The two of them role played an evening together with friends and at a dance. Throughout the entire drama it was apparent that the girl was ashamed of her fat date. She tried to hide him, avoid friends, make believe he was only a casual and unimportant acquaintance and so forth. After the role playing was over the young man commented:

> I was never so self-conscious as in that role playing. I really felt fat and repulsive. Like something people are ashamed of. They don't want to be seen with me. That really brought it home what it means to be real fat.

Practice

All of us who want to change our behavior have fantasies about the way we want to be. If we are "lazy" or "timid," we are likely to visualize situations in which our energy and daring open the way for a new life. In other words fantasy is not a new experience for any of us. We may already daydream a great deal about the way we would like to be and the things we want to do. But despite our imagination we are likely to find ourselves in the same old rut. Why then should fantasy and role playing work now, to help us change our behavior?

Fantasy and role playing work, in contrast to simple daydreaming or wishful thinking, when they are applied in a disciplined way. At the beginning of the chapter we mentioned the investigation of the effect of fantasy on basketball skill. Players who fantasized shooting the ball actually improved their skill when they were later brought on the court and tested. But the fantasy prescribed in the research was not entirely new to the players. Very likely these athletes also had occasional wishful daydreams about how well they played. But these previous fleeting imaginary scenes did not improve their skill because they were fragmentary and haphazard.

In the same way, all our own hopeful visualizations in which we see ourselves as confident, resourceful, libidinous, or successful are not likely to be very effective. These are fantasies but they are casual and unfocused. When we use fantasy and role playing as a method to change our behavior, our mental images must be very specific and must be replayed over and over.

First, as previously mentioned, our fantasies and role playing have to be explicitly detailed. It is no use visualizing to ourselves walking into the boss's office, asking for a raise and getting it. We have to fantasize or role play every possible detail. For example, the man who practiced asking his boss for a raise said that his rehearsals were so real that he saw himself stumbling over a chair in the middle of his employer's office.

The second and very important distinction between casual daydreaming and intentional fantasy and role playing is practice. The basketball players mentally practiced shooting baskets time after time. Roberta practiced inviting the older man on the elevator a total of fourteen times before she actually spoke up. Myrna visualized the terrible consequences of head scratching every morning for two weeks before she really began to curtail her scratching. Once she began to limit her scratching, her program was as follows:

> On the Monday that I was really going to stop scratching I changed my fantasy slightly. For the last two weeks I had just visualized myself scratching and portrayed all the horrible effects in gruesome detail. But on this Monday, after getting up I went to my quiet corner and started concentrating. I saw the consequences again but I also visualized myself stopping completely, only just for that morning. If I did it that morning then all the dreadful things

> I had imagined for two weeks would happen. But if I got through that very morning without scratching, then I was free. I could scratch, do anything, and I was immune. Nothing would happen to me.
>
> From then on, that's how my fantasy went. The horrible things would happen only if I scratched during the forbidden period; which gradually grew from one morning to two mornings, to three and so forth. But if I scratched after the forbidden period my fantasy told me it was OK.

Myrna's fantasy is extremely specific, allows her to reinforce her good behavior, and is continuous. She fantasizes every morning and pictures exactly what will happen. All fantasy and all role playing must be just as frequent, and detailed, if it is to be effective. If you have tried fantasy and it does not seem to work, it may well be that your failure is right along these two dimensions. Be specific and fantasize or role play over and over again.

The value of mental fantasy was vividly brought home to us one spring day on a hike in the ruggedly beautiful Shawangunk Mountains. We were watching a particularly agile man climbing what to us looked pretty much like a sheer eighty-foot cliff. Yet this rock climber was slowly and steadily working his way up, confidently hammering in his pitons and looping his ropes. After his successful climb and descent, we asked how often he had climbed these rocks before. He said he had never made this climb before.

> This is my first time in Shawangunk. I had a climbing book that gives you pictures of the various ascents. But the rest is pure fantasy. I keep myself busy in the winter mentally climbing every rock that I hope to go up in the spring. I must have climbed this one more than fifty times in my mind. I imagine every crack and crevice and I see every toe-hold and where I'll place my pitons. It keeps me amused all winter long and it makes the climb that much easier when I actually get to it.

Conclusion

Fantasy and role playing can lead to very important personality changes. Through fantasy we can rehearse and explore all sorts of possibilities and do so without feeling frightened or inhibited. With the help of role playing, the unresolved doubts and any shortcomings of fantasy can be compensated for. The additional advantage of both is that they are open-ended. Both can lead to new self-understanding and new behaviors. Finally, if, in addition, we combine reinforcement procedures with fantasy, we have a uniquely powerful tool available to us to change our personality and our lives.

Nine
Eating, Smoking, and Drinking

If we are like most people, not only do we want to change some personality traits but we are also not completely satisfied with our eating, drinking, or smoking behavior. Admittedly the majority of adults either eat, drink or smoke more than they want to. We are not now talking about addictions. Those who are actually alcoholics or have medically serious smoking or weight problems need professional help. Surprisingly few persons, however, overindulge to the point where specialized treatment is necessary. For most of us, excessive eating, smoking, or drinking is simply unwanted, conflicted behavior, any one of them can legitimately be called a bad habit. In the preceding chapters the ways in which undesired behaviors can be changed have already been explored. In this chapter we will pull together many of these techniques in order to focus on immoderate habits which are a central problem for many persons.

Abe smokes too much. He is married, a father, and works as a jeweler. Though he has his share of business and personal anxieties, none of his worries is unusual, and he could be considered fairly content. Abe began smoking while in high school and for most of his life has consumed about a pack of cigarettes a day. During the last several years, however, his smoking has increased and he now smokes about two packs a day. His doctor has warned him that a two-pack-a-day habit places him at the risk of serious lung cancer, as well as threatening his heart and blood vessels. Abe has tried to stop several times without success and he is about to give up making any further attempt.

Valerie overeats. She is twenty-four years old, five feet and four inches tall and weighs 156 pounds. She has been married almost a year and in that time, despite well-motivated attempts at dieting, has gained 12 pounds. Over the years she has tried several different diets including the "grapefruit" plan, high protein regimens and medication, but all techniques eventually proved unsuccessful. In each instance, Val stuck to the diet for a few weeks, lost some weight, but then started ignoring the rules and gained again.

Jim drinks excessively. He does not drink very much at home, but at nearly every party he attends he indulges heavily. During the last several years he has managed to find a party nearly every weekend so that he now has an excuse to drink too much several times a month. Jim's marriage is suffering because of his drinking, and he could lose his job too. In addition, his heavy drinking has resulted in two automobile accidents. Despite the fact that his license has been suspended for six months, Jim is still driving and drinking. His past accidents could easily have been serious, but Jim was lucky enough to emerge from both with only minor injuries. It is obvious to all Jim's friends that his continual drinking and driving will ultimately result in tragedy.

Motivation

A critical step before attempting any technique intended to change our personality is to study our motivation. You may recall from Chapter Three that what we call poor willpower is usually nothing more than a hidden need *not* to bring about the personality change we outwardly say we want. Three fairly typical examples of overeating, smoking, and drinking have just been reported. Which of these three persons has failed to change because of conflicting motives?

Abe the heavy smoker seems the least likely to be unconsciously motivated to continue smoking. He is fairly well-adjusted and, like the great majority of smokers, continues his habit because he just does not know effective techniques for breaking it. Val is recently married and gaining more and more weight. She, too, is essentially happy and is sincerely motivated to change her eating behavior. There are no deeply hidden reasons for her snacking and munching; it just always feels so good right then and there, making it very hard to lose weight. Jim on the other hand is a good candidate for motivational conflict. He says he wants to stop his heavy alcohol dependence. He even participated in an excellent alcohol detoxification program but very soon afterwards resumed his drinking. It looks very much as if Jim is unconsciously motivated to continue drinking.

Almost by chance, Jim began an intensive psychotherapeutic relationship. During counseling it became evident that Jim was what is called a suicidal personality. He was one of those persons who, despite a seemingly ordinary exterior, was torn apart inside by severe guilt and self-hatred. Superficially and consciously Jim wanted to stop drinking, but on the inside, unconsciously, he was pushed to continue to drink, drive, and eventually destroy himself.

Before attempting to change any of our eating, drinking, or smoking behavior we need to examine all of our motives, particularly our unconscious needs. Making use of the techniques described in Chapter Three, we have to carefully determine whether our stated wishes to be slim or stop drinking do not actually run counter to drives of which we are not aware. Whenever we spot such powerful unconscious disagreements it is a certainty that even the wisest plans for behavior change will lead nowhere unless we confront and resolve our motivational conflict (Chapter Four). In Jim's case, the outcome was that he ultimately came to grips with his self-destructive wishes through therapy. Jim was raised in a severely punitive home, constantly made to feel guilty and his personality and ambitions ceaselessly disparaged. His father, particularly, poked fun at his intelligence and accomplishments and made him feel that every success was actually a failure for which he needed to repent. The result was that as the adult Jim became more and more successful, he felt increasing guilt and self-hatred. Without his knowing it, his drinking had been the self-punishment so much desired by his unconscious.

Finding the Reinforcers

Closely related to hidden motives that may propel us to drink, eat and smoke more than we really believe we want to, or should, are hidden reinforcers. Our bad habits may be so closely tied to a reward that the undesired behavior is constantly reinforced. As a beginning step in reducing his smoking, Abe was instructed to observe his own cigarette behavior. He found that he smoked mainly while on the job. He seemed particularly to chain smoke when using certain small tools to cor.struct or repair jewelry. He noticed that as his eyes began to tire, or his hands or back ached he smoked more and more. Valerie, the recently married overweight woman, observed that her nibbling increased as the day wore on. Her eating seemed correlated with her daily feelings of boredom and loneliness. If there were no one to talk to, or nothing interesting to do, at least she could eat.

All bad habits persist no matter how much we may sincerely dislike them, if in one way or another they are reinforced. When Val felt unhappy, she ate, watched TV, or read till she felt better. When Abe was tired and achy he took a break, stretched, smoked, and relaxed and this made him feel better. Whenever you want to rid yourself of unwanted behavior, observe yourself so that you can uncover how that behavior is being reinforced. Carefully scrutinize the situations in which you eat, smoke, or drink. How is the unwanted behavior being directly reinforced, or is it linked to other behaviors or consequences that are rewarding? Re-read Chapter Two in order to recall the means to observe and record behavior, and Chapter Five to review how many different ways your actions may be reinforced. The more diligently you search, the more likely you will turn up one or more ways in which your overindulgence is part of a reinforcement pattern that, once it is obvious, readily lends itself to change.

When you find the reinforcers supporting your bad habit, you are ready to take action. When Abe found his smoking tied in with relieving fatigue and tension he substituted chewing gum instead. Now that cigarettes were no longer associated with the good feeling of relaxation he found his need to smoke growing less and less. Val observed her eating interwoven with behaviors intended to relieve her loneliness and boredom, so she set out to disrupt this reinforcement sequence. First, whenever she felt lonely, she tried telephoning friends, figuring this would not only keep her busy but talking would conflict with eating. This was partly successful, but soon Valerie noted that she felt lonely and ate even when her husband was home. Once again, using trial and error, she searched for ways to break up old habit patterns. To relieve her boredom during the day, Val got a part-time job. To resolve her loneliness when her husband was with her, she became more affectionate and physically expressive. Now when she felt blue, she kissed, petted or pampered her husband, as the situation demanded, instead of rushing to the kitchen to eat. Valerie's affection was not always rewarded, but remember, partial reinforcement can powerfully shape behavior.

> Mickey considered himself a "two fisted drinker." He frequented a singles bar, loved parties, and routinely drank after work. But he was also an intelligent and sensitive individual who wanted to enjoy life. He was seriously unhappy about his increasing drinking and was profoundly motivated to change. Mickey carefully observed himself, and with pencil and paper charted his drinking. After several weeks of meticulous record-keeping and detective-like self-scrutiny, he found that his drinking was sexually rewarded. Mickey was shy and found it difficult to approach women. But when he drank he became spontaneous and light-hearted. After a few drinks he was able to flirt, tease, and generally be entertaining in a very convivial way. Drinking permitted Mickey to initiate contact with women and reap all the rewards of sexuality. If he were to stop drinking, Mickey needed to find another way of reaching out to the opposite sex.

Just as drinking rewarded Mickey with sexuality, it may be reinforced in another individual because it permits aggression, relaxation, exhibitionism, or any number of other behaviors that are satisfying. In order to cut down on the drinking that sanctions these behaviors, one must find a substitute for obtaining reinforcement. A commuter who found he drank heavily when he arrived home in order to unwind, substituted a hot bath. A widow who started drinking to "forget" her grief found working as a hospital volunteer much more effective in achieving her goal and far more rewarding. Whenever we want to stop a bad habit, we need to uncover how it is now being reinforced, or reinforcing, and then substitute desired behaviors.

When we investigate the reinforcers for our bad habits, we may find many instances in which there is a situational reinforcement. We may only smoke or drink in certain circumstances and the rewards may not be obvious at all. Betsy, for example, noticed that she smoked whenever she drank coffee. The reason for this association was not very clear, but by drinking less coffee Betsy automatically cut down on her smoking. Now during breaks, Betsy drank juice or a soft drink. Vincent noticed that he drank primarily while watching television. During an evening he could consume six to ten cans of beer while watching TV. Again the reinforcers in this situation were not obvious, and Vincent at first had little success substituting different behaviors. Ultimately, however, Vincent hit on the simple expedient of eating instead of drinking while watching TV. Since Vincent could well afford the extra calories this routine worked for him.

When we are looking for the reinforcers for our undesired behavior we need to carefully study the environment and conditions in which we eat, smoke, or drink excessively. Often to curtail our eating, drinking, or smoking, we need simply to alter the situation. Betsy eliminated a good deal of smoking by eliminating coffee. Vincent substituted another response, eating instead of drinking while watching TV. Careful self-observation will permit us to see all the ways in which our bad habits are tied in to our lives.

> Dr. L. had been a heavy smoker for most of his adult years and was now determined to radically reduce his dependence. He found that his main difficulty was that smoking for him was part of many different situations. He drew up a list of all the settings and stimuli that triggered his smoking. His catalogue included the following linkages: after meals, with coffee, with alcohol, after sex, while driving, studying, reading, during lab work, TV viewing, parties, and conversations. Armed with this information, Dr. L began to systematically eliminate one situation after another. He listed the weakest smoke linkage first, and then went progressively on from there to the strongest. He found that after sex he had the lowest inducement to smoke and after meals the highest. Knowing this, he gradually worked his way up his hierarchy.
>
> Eliminating the first cigarette-linked behavior was easy. Sex induced the least urge to smoke. Now instead of smoking after sex, Dr. L substituted a shower. After securely breaking this connection, Dr. L worked on ridding himself of the next one, smoking while watching television. He never smoked in the kitchen so he moved his viewing into the kitchen, thereby eliminating smoking with an incompatible response. After several weeks the TV-cigarette association was effectively abolished, enabling Dr. L to

work his way further up his hierarchy. Finally, as each smoking linkage was broken Dr. L limited his smoking to a few recreational situations, thus cutting his consumption down to only a few per day.

It is appropriate at this point to comment on the frequent tendency to switch from cigarettes to pipes or cigars when attempting to stop smoking. Such a shift sometimes works. The substitution of other tobacco products, even chewing them, instead of smoking cigarettes, may enable a few persons to moderate their habits. We ourselves, however, have not found such attempts very successful. Even worse, research shows that confirmed cigarette smokers tend to carry their habit of inhaling with them when they switch to pipes or cigars. The consequence of this is that inhaling pipe and cigar smoke may be more hazardous to health than cigarette consumption. For most people hoping to curtail their cigarette use it is best to work directly on the amount consumed daily and not try to reduce by switching over to pipes or cigars.

Reasonable Goals

Don't *stop* drinking or smoking! For healthy adults the goal should *not* be to entirely stop cigarettes or alcohol or slim down till they resemble a Hollywood star. Success in mastering bad habits may be much more likely when the goal is to drink, smoke, or eat in moderation. Frequently one of the most formidable barriers to controlling some unwanted behaviors is that the person believes himself faced with an all or nothing situation. Looking forward to a future of never being permitted a cordial glass of wine with a special dinner forecasts a dreadfully ascetic future for some of us. Faced with such apparently gloomy prospects many individuals give up trying to modify their habits before they even begin.

The goal of moderation, rather than total abstinence, seems to work even with confirmed alcoholics. It is generally believed that a reformed alcoholic should never drink again. Even a single glass of beer with a hot dog is forbidden since it is thought that just the tiniest fraction of alcohol may again start the downward spiral of chronic inebriation. For many ex-alcoholics this may indeed be true so that drinking should be continually avoided.

But it must also be noted that psychologists working with some alcoholics have found surprising success in helping them reach a level of controlled drinking. Instead of being expressly forbidden all alcohol, patients have been successfully taught to drink in moderation. Similar results have been obtained with heavy cigarette smokers. Of course not every heavy smoker or drinker is able to work toward reasonable goals. But we suggest that persons attempting to limit their bad habits, particularly those who have had little success with all-or-none approaches, set their sights a little lower.

> Bob was thirty-four, married, the father of twins, and an architect. After finishing school he had spent several years in New York City where he apparently picked up the habit of drinking a great deal of Scotch and Irish whiskey. As the years went by, his drinking increased to the point where counting lunch, pre-dinner and after-dinner drinks, he consumed about three to six ounces of whiskey daily. Clearly this was a very high level of alcoholic intake, and was beginning to affect both his work and health. During his last medical examination his physician had remarked that Bob's liver appeared slightly enlarged and questioned him about his drinking.
>
> Bob's first attempt to stop drinking was a disastrous failure. He visited with his clergyman who enumerated the evils of liquor, put Bob on a strict diet and asked to be called daily so Bob could affirm that he had not drunk that day. Bob continued with this plan for about twenty days, and then, "exploded like a time bomb, and went on a bender to end all benders." Several other attempts to stay on the wagon followed but none was successful.

Eventually Bob began a personality-change program and set realistic goals for his drinking. He was asked to examine his drinking habits and isolate the reinforcers. He liked alcohol and in fact often bemoaned the fact that he could no longer enjoy wine with his meals because he had indulged in too many whiskies before dinner. In formulating his plan, then, his final goal became to cut out all hard liquor and substitute wine. Drinking with lunch was permitted once a week, and the limited amount of alcohol was to be consumed largely with food. Drinking during dinner was confined to five glasses of wine a week which could be spaced in any reasonable way. To help himself work toward his new goals, Bob became a wine expert, purchased very costly vintages and learned to savor every glassful in a way in which he had never enjoyed whiskey.

Mickey had found drinking enabled him to become outgoing and sexually attractive. But his dependence on alcohol was clearly excessive. He needed to moderate his habits and began what he called a three-pronged attack. If one did not work, surely the other would. First he permitted himself only one singles bar, party, or other alcohol scene per month. Providing he drank only modestly the rest of the time (a daily glass of wine or two, or a mixed drink), during his one monthly break he could pull out all the stops. At the same time, however, Mickey knew that his once-a-month, party-drinking should not result in a spree. Remember, he could only drink enough to become extroverted and not so much that he passed out. If he passed out, nobody would be attracted to him.

Second, Mickey explored nonalcoholic ways of meeting women and feeling relaxed. He eventually discovered a singles hiking club. The casual clothing and joint physical exhaustion quickly enabled men and women to feel at ease with one another. The third possibility was that Mickey decided to look into the possibility of counseling or joining an encounter group. He found two questions about himself he wanted to answer. Why did he actually have to have something like alcohol to loosen him up? Second, why did he need so many new relationships—why didn't some of the old good ones last?

What should the goals be if you want to curtail your own bad habits? For cigarette smokers a good goal is to cut down to about one pack every three or four days. Of course this is done slowly. First, the goal might be to smoke only thirty cigarettes a day, then in a week or so cut down to twenty-five, then twenty, and so forth. It may take several months till the goal is reached but this kind of slow and steady progression is a useful ally. For heavy drinkers, a similar gradual reduction in alcohol consumption is recommended. In addition, greater emphasis should be shifted to wine and beer, with hard liquors de-emphasized. Eventually the goal might be to have a single drink with lunch once or twice a week, limiting this to a single glass or two of wine or the equivalent. Weight watchers should also set their goals much more realistically. A handy rule for how many pounds to lose is to take the weight you want to lose and cut it in half.

Valerie, for example, wanted to lose forty pounds. With the new more reasonable goals in mind she should aim only to lose twenty pounds. This overly simplified rule is, of course, only roughly approximate, but it suggests that dieters be realistic and modest in the goals they set for themselves.

A word about diets. We are not advocates of any particular plan so long as the regimen is well-balanced and nourishing. Any good diet recommended by a doctor or other legitimate authority is likely to be sound, and if followed carefully, weight reducing. The behavior-change plan we suggest is directed toward helping people eliminate snacking, and to stick to their diets. By following the personality-change procedures suggested, individuals can learn to avoid unwise eating and gradually let a good diet become the sole source of food.

Reward Yourself

Very likely the most powerful and effective way to cultivate new behavior is to reward it. Following, then, the procedures just suggested to change your eating, drinking, or smoking, figure out a reinforcement system for your new behavior. You may decide to use tokens, giving yourself a chip each time you successfully resist eating, smoking, or drinking. When you have sufficient chips you can then trade them in for some highly desirable reward. Or you may use money, actually paying yourself.

> In addition to substituting chewing gum for smoking, Abe figured that each cigarette cost him four cents. He assumed that normally he would smoke thirty-five cigarettes a day. Thus when he only smoked twenty cigarettes he awarded himself sixty cents; when he was down to ten cigarettes he paid himself one dollar. By the end of his first month Abe had accumulated $14 which he promised himself to spend frivolously. As the months went by, Abe's reward grew and grew till finally he was earning over $35 monthly.
>
> In addition to the partial reinforcement of affection she got from her husband, Valerie rewarded her diet behavior by buying a special bit of clothing whenever she reached her weight goal. Her objective was to lose two pounds every month. She weighed herself on the last day of each month, in the morning before breakfast. If Val reached her objective she was allowed to spend up to fifty dollars of her own earned money on clothing that she would not otherwise buy.

The range of rewards is endless. One former heavy smoker found it satisfying to have his wife affectionately squeeze his hand whenever she detected he was not smoking at a party, during a conversation, after dinner or in any of the situations in which he usually lit up. Another smoker rewarded herself by stroking and caressing her hair whenever she resisted the urge to smoke. This may in itself not be the most desirable habit but it is far less harmful than heavy smoking. A dieter used a very effective reward, but one that must be administered sparingly, and that is food itself. Whenever he attained his monthly weight goal he was allowed one food splurge. Since his favorite food was pie with ice cream he worked diligently to lose two pounds monthly so he could enjoy his richly longed-for extravagance. The reward you choose for yourself is limited only by your imagination. So long as it is truly appealing and you don't cheat, it can be a very effective way to encourage new behavior in place of old undesired conduct.

Punishment

Punishment, as we have seen in Chapter Six, can be used to help change behavior but, admittedly, it is often a difficult and uncertain technique. In the hands of experts punishment may work very well, but when we attempt to use it ourselves, we may become so disenchanted with the entire process that we give up even trying to eat, drink, or smoke less. Thus we suggest that punishment techniques be used only as a last resort and then with extreme caution. First try everything we have described. If these methods do not work, then perhaps you may try self punishment cautiously.

The simplest form of punishment is to make an unwanted behavior painful. This has been done for smokers by providing an electrified cigarette case. The case contains a battery which delivers a powerfully uncomfortable shock whenever a cigarette is withdrawn. A similar type of punishment was devised by a businesswoman who wanted to cut down drastically on her drinking. She had always disliked tomato juice, finding its taste bitter and its texture nauseating. In order, therefore, to punish her drinking she insisted on forcing herself to sip tomato juice whenever she had alcohol. At business lunches and dinners she ordered only Bloody Marys and at home she forced herself to drink a full glass of juice *immediately after* she had alcohol. Even more drastic and seriously painful punishment of drinking can be accomplished with Antabuse, a drug that produces severe gastro-intestinal symptoms when ingested along with alcohol.

Self punishment may also be used to curtail eating. One woman attached a box to her refrigerator which required a one dollar donation everytime it was opened for improper eating. A more common and sometimes effective technique is to couple unwise eating with a fantasy punishment (Chapter Eight). Imaginary punishment works as follows.

1. Imagine the worst consequences of eating. For some persons, this would be visualizing themselves fat, ugly, and alone. For one woman her worst imaginary punishment was remembering the sight of her very overweight mother collapsing and dying of a heart attack. At a family picnic the mother playfully chased her young, and first, grandchild. Suddenly she screamed and collapsed. "I see my mother lying in a heap. She is holding her chest. I see the fear and awful pain in her eyes. We're all terrified. She is struggling to breath. She is in agony and she dies."

2. After your punishing image is intense and potent, think of the foods associated with your fantasy. Visualize the cakes, creams, candy, fats, and sugars that will produce the obese, undesirable, vulnerable, and unhealthy person you do not wish to be. Let yourself get angry, get disgusted at these foods. The woman whose image was that of her obese mother dying of heart failure said, "I think of my mother's pain and agony together with what made her so fat. I think of rich desserts and fatty meat and omelets and I feel a wave of nausea come over me. I feel as if when these things are presented to me I will throw up." Let the unpleasant emotions build. Let yourself feel angry, sick, or afraid when you see undesired foods.

3. When you feel powerfully negative, decisively relieve the bad image by replacing it with a good fantasy. You are eating a healthy salad, a lean broiled steak, and you are trim and attractive. Your fantasy is positive and good.

4. In an actual food situation, as soon as you see the undesired foods or are tempted to eat unwisely, immediately call up your

punishing fantasy. Actually feel repelled, disgusted, and infuriated by the foods you do not want. Then move quickly away while you still have the bad feeling and get ready to shift. As desirable eating comes into view, take hold of the good fantasy and feel proud and well.

Using this technique, an interior decorator seriously overweight for twenty-five years, was able to reduce successfully for the first time in his life.

> My fantasy is built around my father who had a stroke when he was fifty-four. He was big and he was fat. I see his arteries clogged with fat as I remember him sitting in his wheelchair. His eyes are sunken and he drools because he has lost control of his muscles. When I see that image of what could happen to me, I actually become afraid of fattening foods. I literally can tremble at the idea of having to eat something full of saturated fats and calories.
>
> When I'm out, say like in a cafeteria and I see the french fries and pork chops and cream-filled desserts I let the fantasy come over me. I see my father, incapacitated and helpless and I get mortally afraid. I won't touch those foods. Then I reward myself by moving away quickly. You have to do it fast otherwise the foods themselves can capture you. You know, you might start thinking maybe there isn't that much to be afraid of. That kind of thing. So very fast while I am still holding on to my fear fantasy I go over to the salads. Now I let the good image come to me. I take the salad, I am slim and youthful. I play tennis and I feel good.

There is one more punishment method that should be mentioned but *not* recommended. Granted the technique may work, but it too often has undesirable results. It is one of the oldest punishment tools which in one turn-of-the-century book on child care is called "exhaustion." Mothers are instructed that if a child has a bad habit such as nail biting or blinking then they may cure it by forcing the child to bite or blink till he is literally exhausted. The punishment here consists of the continual repetition of the undesired act to the point where it is extremely painful. This has been tried with cigarette smoking and eating too. The smoker is instructed to smoke pack after pack till he is sick and exhausted. The person that wants to diet is forced to stuff himself with food till he is in actual pain. By logical extension the immoderate drinker should then be forced to drink till he is unconscious, something which many do anyway without any beneficial effect. This technique of punishing oneself with the bad habit itself surfaces now and again in magazines or texts, but we mention it only to *caution against its use*.

Conclusion

Not only can we change our personality but using the same methods we can control our eating, smoking, and drinking behavior. First we need to clearly understand our motives and neutralize any unconscious conflicting drives blocking our progress. Second, it is necessary to detect and change the often subtle ways in which our present overeating, drinking, or smoking may be part of a complex reinforcement pattern. Once we understand the ways in which our overindulgence is rewarding, we can substitute more suitable behaviors. It is important also to be thoroughly realistic about our goals. Self-directed behavior-change techniques are not likely to cure addictions but can help us moderate eating, drinking, and smoking so that they are enjoyable activities and not bad habits. Finally, if nothing else works, direct self punishment can sometimes be effective. We should realize, however, that the persistence of the bad habit is often punishment enough and we might be far more effective in changing if instead of punishing the bad we rewarded the good behaviors we want to establish.

Ten
Gaining
Friends
and
Changing
Others

In our quest for better lives, it is often not enough just to change our own personalities. We do not live in isolation; we require the acceptance and warmth of others. Even if we are married or belong to a family, we still need friends with whom to share experiences and exchange intimate feelings. With the techniques we have already learned, plus some new ones, we can work towards two new, personal, goals. First we will learn how to satisfy our quest for friends, and simultaneously become aware of how to deepen our present relationships. Second, we will learn to bring about desirable changes in the behavior of other people, often almost entirely without their knowing they themselves are changing.

Listen Responsively

The first step in gaining friendships requires that we alter our own behavior. Specifically we need to learn to listen in an active, intensive way that we have never before experienced. Of course the instruction to *listen* sounds deceptively easy. You may assert that you have been listening to other people all of your life. We disagree, for we have found that most people actually listen very little. In practice, most persons who think they are listening are usually just biding their time, impatiently waiting their turn, interrupting, or making irrelevant comments. Instead of listening in the manner we call *responsive*, they listen intrusively. They continuously intrude their egotistical demands, questions, and disagreements. Here is a typical conversation. June is trying to tell Jack something that she feels is very important to her. Jack, an average listener, hears and understands very little of what June is hoping to communicate.

June: *So as I was saying he came in and was acting very quiet-like so I was wondering—*

Jack: *He never acts quiet. He couldn't really have been quiet.*

June: *Well he was! So anyway I sat down preparing for something way out. I had that strange feeling you get—*

Jack: *You're always feeling strange. Get to the point!*

June: *I am! Will you shut up!*

Jack: *I'm not saying anything. You're just telling me another pointless story.*

June: *All right! I'm telling you what he said. But it scared me the way he came out with it. He said he was moving out! Out and away and —*

Jack: *Big deal! It's not the first time.*

June: *I know it's not, but it's me. Don't you see how this is af-fecting me? It's got me so that—*

Jack: *I wonder whether he would want to sell his rugs. Did he say anything about that?*

June: *I don't know! And I don't care!*

Jack: *What are you acting so huffy about? I'm sitting here listening to you tell me all this bull, so who cares.*

June: *Well it's obvious you don't.*

Unfortunately a great deal of what passes for listening to another is little better than the example above. Many of us rarely listen responsively and as a consequence really hear or under-stand little of what is being said. Even worse, our inattentive, egotistical listening tells our friends we do not really care about them. To listen responsively first of all requires that we signal our attention and encourage the other person to continue. By saying "mm hm," by nodding our head, or saying "yes," "yup" or the equivalent, we indicate that we are attending and want them to go on. Try it! You may know someone with whom you would like to be friendly but have never managed to talk very much with them. Set aside a convenient relaxed time to listen to them. Just encourage whatever your acquaintance is saying by nodding or interjecting "mm hm." What you are doing is reinforcing the other person's verbal behavior. And as we know from Chapter Five, behavior that is reinforced persists.

The first and most important step in building a friendship is to encourage the other person to talk to you. This requires that you yourself completely desist from remarks that are critical, diversionary or disruptive. Instead you reinforce the other individual's conversation by nodding or otherwise signaling that you are listening fully. When this kind of reinforcement has sufficiently encouraged the other's conversation, you may then responding by restating, in a summary way, what has been said. Notice you do not have to agree with what your friend is saying but your synopsis has to indicate that you have been listening and understanding.

Igor: *I told my brother that I just can't lend him any more money. I can't afford it.*

Van: *You've lent him as much as you can.*

Igor: *Right. I have responsibilities to my family. My wife had a gall bladder operation. Both my kids have a terrific dental bill. And he keeps building one version after another of that damn car. And nobody will buy it.*

Van: *Mm hm.*

Igor: *It's wasted money. I had four thousand dollars I could call my own when he started borrowing. Now I got five hundred in the bank. That's not much for a family man. It doesn't cover two weeks if I was out of work.*

Van: *You've lent him as much as you reasonably could.*

Igor: *The only way I could see his ever making his machine work would be if he started to show it around the country. That doesn't take much. He would get a lot of free exhibition space at fairs and things, you know.*

Van: *You believe he could show it around and it wouldn't have to cost anything?*

Igor: *Yeah! That's how it's done. Publicity and it's free. Meanwhile I can feel that my money is my own for a change.*

Van: *It would free you of the burden of having to finance him.*

Igor: *Right! I didn't tell you the big part. My wife has put her foot down. She's practically said in so many words that it's my brother and the car or it's her and the family.*

Van: *Yes, I see.*

Van has encouraged his friend to talk more and more freely simply by indicating he was listening ("mm hm") and restating what Igor has said. As a result Igor begins to explore some of his confused feelings, at which point Van uses a third technique. He now helps his friend by reflecting feeling. Notice that Van does not state his own emotions. He listens and tries to understand the emotions that Igor is conveying, and verbalize, or reflect, these feelings.

Igor: *I'll admit it. It has me confused. I mean it is my brother and he is not a mad scientist. I have to help him. And it is my own family and I have got to think of them.*

Van: *You feel you have a conflict and you don't know how to act.*

Igor: *I feel torn this way and that. It has given me a lot of sleepless nights. I get very blue, feel real down.*

Van: *It makes you depressed.*

Igor: *Very. I mean it puts me in a quandary. If my wife could be more understanding. Like if she wasn't so mad about the money. I think she could be more objective. She likes my brother and all. But she is giving us a hard time.*

Van: *I sense maybe you are a little mad at her. She could be more sympathetic.*

Igor: *Yeah! I think that's it. She could be more on my side. I am trying to do the right thing. I have her best interest in mind. I wish she could see that.*

Using the three responsive listening techniques, Van has permitted his friend to unburden himself. He is not necessarily agreeing with Igor, nor taking the wife's or brother's side. Neither is Van waiting to pounce on his friend with advice on how to solve his problems. The role of a good friend is not that of a psychotherapist. True friends are people who help us get things off our chest. They may not be able to supply answers but they do listen, encourage us to develop our own story and untangle our feelings.

In summary, listening responsively requires that we stop old intrusive listening behaviors and instead substitute new responsive ones. Whenever we intend to listen to someone, there should be no interruptions, no restless waiting our turn to talk, no contradictions, no gratuitous advice. Instead we should *reinforce* the flow of speech by saying "mm hm," indicate our understanding by *restatement* and help clarify our friend's emotions by *reflecting* feeling. Doing these things in the process of listening responsively is of itself often sufficient to start a close friendship.

Disclosing Self

The person you want to be friendly with has started to like you. You are such a good listener. In fact you listen so responsively that your new friend has hardly noticed how little you really say. Before he does notice it, the time has come (once your friend has finished talking) to start to deepen your relationship by revealing yourself. Friendships, all joint human relationships, require reciprocity. Both members of a pair give and take. Your friend who has revealed himself also wants to know you. To start your self disclosure, it is often easiest to describe your background. Telling who you are and where you are from is an acceptable conversational introduction that is nonthreatening. Learning your background enables your friend to feel a little more trust now that your identity is becoming clear. The following is an excerpt from a conversation of a young man who has just met a woman at a party. She is appealing to him and he wants to have her like him. The man has tried responsive listening, but since the woman is quite shy and the party situation somewhat intimidating, he has not been able to encourage her to say very much. To put her at ease he talks about his background.

> You look very Armenian to me. You probably are not, I guess; there are very few Armenians in the city actually. But you know, your dark eyes and the way you have your hair— my grandmother was Armenian and as a child she would tell me stories about her country. It sounded so beautiful. The woods, and old stucco houses. Everybody had a few chickens and a cow. I grew up in the city, went to college

here and everything. So I have always had a soft spot, you know, for beautiful country and woods. In my office (I'm an industrial engineer), I have these enlarged photos of some of the pictures my grandmother brought with her. They were passed on to my parents. My father used to keep them in his store. Now I keep them in my office. They make me feel better about working there.

This disclosure of background is not very intimate. Highly personal details are omitted, deliberately, for they would not be appropriate in this setting, nor on a first occasion. Later on when the conversation has progressed, or the relationship developed, more revealing background details are gradually called for. During their second meeting, for example, this man told more about his parents and how their strict disciplinarian standards caused him to be a very fearful and awkward adolescent.

Following the disclosure of background, and sometimes along with it, feelings should be revealed. Now you talk with your new friend about your hopes, emotions, plans, aspirations and frustrations. Again, at the beginning, the disclosure is not very personal. If you talked about your innermost fears, conflicts or neuroses as soon as you met a potential friend you would more than likely scare them away. Disclosure of feelings early in a relationship is generally superficial but as the relationship develops it becomes more and more intimate. Here is the same young man three weeks later, talking with the woman whom he met at the party. He has seen her five times since the party and a good friendship seems to be developing. His disclosure of feeling might be said to be at an intermediate level, not superficial but not yet intensively deep either.

I may look relaxed but I am not really easygoing. I know that. I work hard at things. I wasn't satisfied with just passing grades. I had to have A's, you know. And I work hard at my job. I am demanding of others too. I'm not unpleasant about it. Don't get me wrong. But I know I'm one of those who has high motivation. I'm an achiever. I wondered about you, you know. You seemed so reserved, and I wondered whether you could relate to someone with a lot of energy. [Friend indicates he is to continue.] Well, I make friends but I also scare a lot of them off. I am working on that part of myself. I'm going to keep on being an

achiever but I don't want it to cost me good friendships. I'm
getting to know myself better, a little anyway.

Talking about your background and disclosing more and
more of your feelings is a demonstration to your new friends, or
old ones, that you value and trust them. You have encouraged
them to talk to you and in the process they have revealed more
and more of themselves. Now you are responding by telling
about yourself. Both of you share a new intimacy, a fresh understanding and rapport that makes for satisfying friendship.

Changing Others

By responsive listening and self disclosure we are, in effect,
changing the behavior of others. When we select other persons
(who also select us) to listen to responsively and portion out
background information to, we are indirectly altering their
personalities. Once they were distant and strange but we have
helped them come closer and like us. We can also work directly
and intentionally on changing someone else's personality. We can
single out specific characteristics we want to increase, or decrease, and using the same behavior change procedures we
employed on ourselves, shape the actions of others.

The simplest and most potent tool we have for changing the
behavior of others is reinforcement (see Chapter Five). At the
beginning of this chapter we saw how just a subtle "mm hm"
encourages another's speech. Using the same "mm hm" as the
reinforcer, psychological researchers have brought about all sorts
of remarkable alterations in behavior. Some investigators reinforced physical mannerisms such as head scratching or chin
stroking. Other researchers reinforced the use of certain words
such as the pronouns *we* or *I*. In other words, subjects who
thought they were simply conducting an ordinary conversation,
were actually having specific behaviors reinforced by the investi-
gator saying "mm hm." In all such instances, head scratching,
using the word *I*, or other selected behaviors continuously
showed significant increases. Most important of all, none of the
subjects knew that any of their behavior increased through reinforcement. *Behavior change, through reinforcement, takes place
without the subject's awareness.*

Mary complained that though her husband seemed to love her and they were happily married, he was not very affectionate or "physical." When asked to specify the behaviors she wanted to see in her husband, Mary stated that she wanted him to touch more frequently. She felt that he rarely kissed her, patted her, or held her hand. During coitus, she also complained, he did not hug, stroke, or pet sufficiently.

Mary had several times complained to her husband that he was insufficiently "physical" but the talks had little positive effect. Mary's counselor was familiar with behavior change techniques and asked her to think of something she could do that would act as a reinforcer for her husband. Mary thought of all sorts of rewards ranging from tokens to food but none seemed practical or appropriate for intimate physical contact. Finally with a little embarrassment, Mary mentioned that her husband liked to hear her "purr" or "moan" with satisfaction. These pleasurable "mmm" sounds seemed an excellent reinforcer. Mary was instructed, therefore, to always reward a good physical contact with a pleasurable "mmm.'" For simple physical contacts a little purr was sufficient but for more extensive ones a more rewarding "mmm" could be forthcoming. Mary was afraid her husband would know what she was doing but she was reassured that appropriate reinforcement would not be noticed.

At first Mary's attempt to change her husband's behavior did not make much progress. The difficulty was that Mary's husband so rarely made adequate physical contact that there were too few opportunities for reinforcement. When this was discovered Mary was asked to prime the pump. She was told to help her husband do the patting and petting she wanted, and then to reward him. Once Mary helped her husband do some of the touching she wanted, and then reinforced this behavior, her husband's physical expressiveness grew rapidly.

Sometimes the behavior we want in another is almost totally absent. We may desire that the other person say yes more frequently, or touch us, or be more "generous," but there are almost no instances of any of these behaviors. In such cases we have to help the behavior to occur so that we can begin encouraging it through reinforcement. Mary took her husband's hand and started it stroking her. Then she "purred" the reinforcing "mmm" sounds. A husband who wanted his wife to be more agreeable asked questions and made suggestions to which he was certain his wife would answer yes. Then he strongly reinforced these positive agreements. Eventually through careful pump-priming and consistent reinforcement, he got her to the point where she was far more agreeable than even he had suspected was possible. And all of this happened without the wife's being aware that she was being reinforced and her behavior changed.

When we set about to change another's behavior we need to remember not only to reinforce what we do want, but also to stop reinforcing what we do not desire. You may recall from Chapter Five how many subtle ways our own actions can reward, and thus strengthen, undesirable responses. The child scolded for eating with his fingers may really be being urged to continue his bad habits since the scolding can be a reinforcer. In the following example a mother complained that her daughter did not confide in her. She wanted more intimacy between them.

> Mrs. E. is thirty-seven years old and has been divorced for six years. She lives with her seventeen-year-old-daughter, her only child. While the relationship between the two is more or less adequate, Mrs. E. feels she is being "shut out" of her daughter's life. "Mary Ellen almost never tells me anything. If she goes to a dance and I ask how it was she say's "OK" and that's the end of that. I just know one or two names of her friends. And only first names at that. I want her to sit down with me and talk with me. I can help her, I'm sure. I went through a lot of things myself when I was her age. I'm not an old fogey yet."

An analysis of the interaction between mother and daughter showed that often as not Mrs. E actually reinforced her daughter's silence. Typically she asked about a party, or a friend and her daughter said almost nothing. Then to "fill in the silence," the mother would start talking about her own adolescence or some of her more immediate social concerns. Apparently the daughter enjoyed hearing about her mother. Consequently the mother was reinforcing her daughter's silence.

Mrs. E was instructed to seldom ask her daughter a question and never, never to reinforce her daughter's silence or short answer. When her daughter did start talking about her friends and her concerns, Mrs. E was told to use the techniques of responsive listening which are themselves reinforcing. When her daughter was completely finished, Mrs. E was to additionally reward her daughter by telling her about her own life.

Mrs. E was able to extinguish her daughter's silence by no longer reinforcing it. Instead she reinforced the behavior she wanted. A similar situation arose for Nelly who wanted her friend to stop smashing tennis balls over the net. With increasing frequency her friend hit the balls harder and harder. Studying the interaction, Nelly found she was reinforcing this "smashing" behavior by always remarking, "Wow," or commenting on her opponent's skill. To eliminate these hard returns, all Nelly had to do was stop commenting or reacting to powerful volleys. Instead whenever the ball sailed over nicely she complimented by saying "good," thus reinforcing more desired tennis behavior. Again, despite Nelly's doubts, her friend's behavior was changed without his noticing why Nelly was saying "good"; while one behavior was being extinguished, another was being reinforced.

Sometimes when we are confronted with another's behavior that we would like to change, we are unable to pinpoint a solution in terms of reinforcement or extinction. Perhaps we cannot isolate the specific behaviors in a situation that we want to alter. Or maybe we do not understand our own motivation. Whenever another's personality makes us uncomfortable but behavior planning does not seem appropriate, it is time for an *analysis of interaction*. We need to sit down with the other person, and really try to uncover what it is we and they are doing that does not work right.

> Chippy and Kelly are roommates. Chippy is a student nurse and Kelly a part-time actress. They have been living together for a year and a half. Over the last two months both have become increasingly short-tempered with one another. Kelly has complaints about her roommate's lack of neatness and her carelessness in meeting bills. Chippy is unhappy with Kelly's irregular hours and the people that visit her. Through a friend, both become aware of the need for them to patiently analyze what was happening between them.

Kelly: *I found that the main problem was that Chippy and I had become very close, personal friends. More than roommates.*

Chippy: *We had a lot of feeling between us and depended upon each other. When Kelly was down I was there and she was there when I needed her.*

Kelly: *Anyway we really let our hair down, finally. Since nothing seemed to work to make things better we decided to be totally open and honest. We talked through all our complaints about each other and we found that what was happening was jealousy.*

Chippy: *It was hard for me to admit it to Kelly. First I had to admit it to myself. We wrestled with all sorts of differences and problems that weren't really real, just to avoid me facing my jealousy.*

Kelly: *It actually took a couple of weeks. We set aside a regular time every night that we were both home and we would analyze what each of us was doing.*

Chippy: *It became obvious to me that I was being very jealous. I had Kelly all to myself till she got the theater job in October and then she started to bring home her new friends. It was plain I was jealous.*

Kelly: *Once we got that in the open we could deal with it.*

Chippy: *That opened us both up. We were able to really talk to each other about how we felt, and what we wanted.*

Kelly: *We talked about our expectations. We didn't make demands on one another but we did tell what we wanted. You know, what I can give and what Chippy can and all. We labeled our emotions, jealousy, anger, dependency and that. We said what we wanted—to feel care, be supported, and we laid everything bare.*

Kelly and Chippy, through their talks, have moved into what can become the deepest level of friendship. When two persons, whether spouses, lovers, business partners, or just good friends together analyze their interaction, they are equipped to build a progressively deeper and more satisfying relationship. Now each can let the other know what she honestly wants, and together they can work out mutually agreeable accommodations.

The following is an example of what the revealing of some very deeply buried feeling did for a couple who wanted to improve their marriage. The wife related the story. She mentioned that her husband, Phil, had always been a very "sensual" person and that during the first seven years of marriage she had learned to enjoy her own sexualtiy through him. Gradually, however, Phil had become more and more flirtatious with other women. Being familiar with behavior change techniques, the wife had at first tried reinforcement. At a party when her husband was flirting she ignored him and his behavior. But when he was attentive to her she reinforced him by smiling, offering him food, and complimenting him.

> None of my reinforcement efforts worked. It was obvious he got more reward from flirting with somebody else than just my smiling at him. So eventually we got around to discussing it. I mean seriously because before I had mentioned it and he had just tossed it off lightly. Nothing had really been said.
>
> We went away for a weekend to attend an exhibition his company had put on. But we had a lot of time alone so I took advantage of that time together, and we got into a heavy talk the last night. I told Phil that I could see he was attracted to other women and I wanted him to tell me about it. I promised I was not going to reproach him or scold him or act hurt and such. He made the same promise to me.
>
> We began by admitting our fantasies to each other. I did not think I had any, but after Phil told me his dreaming about being intimate with other women, and more than one at a time, mine started to pour out. We discovered a sex gold mine in our fantasies. Anyway, that started the ball rolling. What it came down to was that we were both human and wanted some variety in our sex lives. Phil wanted to be able to have another woman and still have me love him. He did not want an affair, he just wanted to have healthy, pleasurable sexual fun. We love each other and were finally able to admit to ourselves and each other that maybe outside experience should not be forbidden to us.

In order for analysis of interaction to go foward it must be free of recrimination and scolding. If Phil's wife had chastized him as soon as he hinted at his need for more sexual experience, very little would have come of this analysis. Both partners will be frank and straightforward only if they are reassured that their *openness will not be punished*. Putting it more precisely: each partner must *reinforce the other's honesty*. Scoldings, tears, name calling, and the like are not reinforcements. They are punishments that will assure the partner's clamming up.

A good analysis of interaction also requires accurate observation and labeling. Chippy and Kelly carefully studied their situation. How and why were they, once compatible roommates, now irritated with one another. Both carefully observed their interactions and specified the activities and situations, which all pointed to jealousy. Nelly observed that despite her apparent displeasure she was actually reinforcing her tennis partner's smashing returns. Phil and his wife had observed their interactions long enough to clearly label the fact that Phil seemed erotically aroused by other women. All good analysis of interaction requires, as a prerequisite, that we investigate what is happening. Before we jump into an analysis we have to know what behaviors and feelings concern us and specifically label them.

If Phil's wife had not targeted the specific party behavior she worried about, all that might have resulted was a growing and chronic anger. If she had been like a good many wives, or husbands, she would never have articulated her displeasure but merely picked an argument about some irrelevancy, after each party. Instead Phil's wife patiently observed until she was able to state that her husband's flirting made her both jealous and also seemed to arouse her in a very curious sort of way. For his part Phil scrutinized himself well enough to know that his flirting could not be rationalized away as meaningless. He made himself aware of his full motivation and was able to describe it honestly when the appropriate moment arrived. When we are able to describe our feelings and behavior, together analyze our mutual or reciprocal frustrations and desires, the closest, most rewarding level of human friendship has been reached.

Conclusion

We can change our own personality and that of others by specific techniques, which we can use also to add new friends or intensify our relations with old ones. We must not however, act as if our new understanding about personality and behavior has given us secret and powerful tools to manipulate people. This caution attains special importance when we use methods such as responsive listening and self-disclosure to win new friends. As each friendship progresses, our companions should gradually be made aware of what we have learned and what we are doing. The honesty of our feelings for others as well as the ethical commitments mentioned in the first chapter necessitate that, whenever appropriate, we *share* our knowledge and techniques. Giving to others what we ourselves have learned helps all personalities to grow and all our lives to change.

Index